GOD'S WILL > YOUR PLAN

Lessons from Jonah on Embracing your Call, Purpose, and Identity

Jody Moore

Sermon To Book
www.sermontobook.com

God's Will > Your Plan / Jody Moore
ISBN-13: 9780692505267
ISBN-10: 0692505261

To my four children: Marcquel, Kamryn, Raegan, and Bailee Moore. My earnest prayer is that you, too, will live from a place of vocational call and identity.

To my great-grandmother Mama Lula, and my grandmother Veaggie Eppright. I look forward to seeing you in glory.

CONTENTS

A Note from the Author

Hello, and thank you for purchasing *God's Will > Your Plan*. Accompanying each main chapter of the book is a workbook section with a set of reflective questions.

These questions serve as practical tools to help you get the most out of the book so that you can truly submit to God's incredible plan for your life—and survive the big fish that come along to swallow you whole.

After the questions for discussion or reflection, each workbook section concludes with a practical action step.

I recommend you go through these sections with a pen in order to write your thoughts in the areas provided.

You are welcome to go through the questions by yourself, with a friend, or with a study group. Regardless, it is my hope that you enjoy the book thoroughly and grow from the experience!

Pastor Jody Moore

Change on the Horizon

Have you ever had a real and powerful feeling that God is up to something? You can't articulate it or even wrap your head around it, but it's a genuine feeling—one that cannot be denied or ignored.

The fact that you have this book in your hands right now is no accident.

God speaks to us in a number of ways: through our church leaders, through our ministry, through sermons, through Christian books, and even through Bible stories that we grew up hearing in Sunday school.

Take the story of Jonah, for instance. It's a short book—only four chapters long—but can God still use it to speak to His people? Can He use it to inspire change? Of course He can.

The fact that you have this book in your hands right now is no accident. He has a plan and a purpose, and you are part of it. This book is part of it. And that strange, undeniable feeling you've had deep in your spirit, telling you that something big is on the horizon—yes, that's a part of it as well.

In 2007, I preached a series of messages to my parish based on the story of Jonah. I have to be very frank here: I did not know that God would use what I thought would be simplistic sermons to change the life and fabric of the church I pastor.

Little did I know that God would use the story of Jonah to change my life and the ministry ethos of my church.

See, I had just finished preaching a yearlong sermon series on Jesus's Sermon on the Mount. These were some deep, penetrating, and at times sobering messages. When we finished the series, we were all mentally and emotionally exhausted from the weightiness of Christ's words to us. So, after some time in prayer, I decided that something "light" was in order for the house. I would preach through the Book of Jonah.

We would learn a little about God's call on this prophet's life, his flight from that call, and his being swallowed up by a fish. The Lord would speak, but we would have a bit of fun in the process.

Little did I know that God would use the story of Jonah to change my life and the ministry ethos of my church.

Our church has never been the same, and I pray that the same revelation God gave to me for Praise Tabernacle Bible Church of the City of Chino, California, will penetrate the fabric of your heart and soul to bring about the fruit of vocational call and obedience in your life.

Introduction Notes

CHAPTER ONE

God's Call to Purpose

Now the LORD had prepared a great fish to swallow up
Jonah. And Jonah was in the belly of the fish three days
and three nights.

— Jonah 1:17 KJV

I truly believe that God's people are on the edge of a major paradigm shift. There is a change on the horizon that will alter the way His people think and act, and it will reach into every aspect of our lives. It will change how ministry is done and alter the whole complexion of the church. It is a call to purpose, a call to destiny. And it is happening now.

The word "paradigm" refers to a framework—a template of sorts—for how God's people should live and go about their daily lives. Each and every person on the face of this planet has a divine objective, a role to play in God's great plan.

This is our intended destiny. But in order to reach that destiny, we must be open to living out our ordained purpose. There has to be a willingness to move from just *doing* church and going through the motions to *being* the church in truth.

Many of us have had the experience of going to a church service where it all clicks. The lights, the music, the message, the fellowship—they all come together into a joyful, synchronized experience. No one misses a cue, and everyone sings in perfect harmony. There's nothing wrong with that. But God wants more.

Where there's growth, there's change. But growth also necessitates a degree of pain and discomfort.

God wants to move His church beyond the details. God wants to change the identity of His people. He doesn't just want you to *belong* to a church—He wants you to *be* the church.

To Grow or Not to Grow

This paradigm shift that God is orchestrating is happening on a spiritual level. It's up to us, His children, to bring it into the physical realm. In order to do that, God wants us to grow up. He wants us to mature in the Spirit. But no growth ever occurs without a few growing pains.

Where there's growth, there's change. But growth also necessitates a degree of pain and discomfort. Those are scary words. Nobody likes the idea of pain. Most of us do our best to avoid it. Still, in order to become the people God wants us to be, we must accept that there will be growing pains.

We are given the perfect example of this in Christ. Christ Himself suffered before He died and rose again. He had to experience pain to bring about the spiritual growth needed for our salvation.

We are intended to be physically and spiritually the body of Christ.

We are the body of Christ. That is who God intended us to be. Even though Christ ascended into heaven and is seated at the Father's right hand, He is physically present in a very unique and mysterious way on Earth through God's church. We are the legs, the arms, the feet, the very face of Christ upon this Earth. His heart is our heart, His mind is our mind. As Paul reminds us, "Let this mind be in you, which was also in Christ Jesus..." (Philippians 2:5 KJV).

That short verse tells us that God fully expects us to take on the identity of Christ. However, in order to do so and achieve our true purpose, we too will encounter trouble and pain.

We are intended to be physically and spiritually the body of Christ. It is through us that Jesus Himself still walks the dust of the earth. That is a hard concept to grasp. If we look at our actions throughout the course of a week, can we honestly say we did all things as Christ Himself would have done?

This is where the paradigm shift comes in. This is why God wants to inspire growth within our spirit. Without that growth—without that shift in perspective— we cannot embrace our true purpose.

This identity, to which God calls us, will change us from within; but even more so, it will change the world around us.

Each and every one of us is called to fulfill an identity that supersedes and transcends the earthly identity given to us at birth. This identity, to which God calls us, will change us from within; but even more so, it will change the world around us. It is the beginning of a revolution.

Who We Are vs. What We Do

Most Christians understand, at least on some level, that their lives are rooted in Christ, and that their lives are defined by what He did to secure their salvation. But God wants us to take our understanding of this relationship to a more intimate level. He wants us to understand that we are the body of Christ. That is the key to understanding our true identity.

Grasping this concept will move your life in an entirely new direction as a Christian. It will affect how you live, how you work, what you do, and what you don't do. It will seep into every aspect of your life.

This is exciting, but also a little intimidating. Why? The identity that we have as the body of Christ is often in conflict with the earthly identity to which we're accustomed. The things that I might want to do don't necessarily coincide with the things that Christ would do.

But the true joy, the true paradigm shift, occurs when we truly accept our identity in Christ. Then His desires become our desires.

We are all born into flesh that is self-seeking. We want to do things that bring us pleasure and what we think is joy. But shifting our perspective and allowing ourselves to take on our true identity as the body of Christ means we have to do things that please God, not ourselves.

Our earthly selves take second seat, so to speak, to our divine nature. Many people find that a scary notion. After all, no one wants to be second. We all want our needs and desires to be met.

But the true joy, the true paradigm shift, occurs when we truly accept our identity in Christ. Then His desires become our desires. The conflict ceases and we are ready to live our lives fully clothed in our new identity.

However, this creates a paradox. We as Christians want to live a life that is supernatural, yet the lives we lead are often led by flesh.

One of the biggest delusions we are under today as Christians is that our lives are shaped by our circumstances. That is a lie! Our lives are shaped by our identity in Christ. You are not defined by your job, or your social status, or what car you drive, or how many kids you have, or who your spouse is. To live that way is to deny your true self.

God will move in your life, and you will live your life with intentionality and purpose.

Rather, you are defined by Christ and by your purpose as the body of Christ here on this earth. That fact alone changes everything. And once you truly grasp that concept, the supernatural will take charge.

God will move in your life, and you will live your life with intentionality and purpose. Until then, life will continue to be an impossible struggle to attain the supernatural through natural, earthly means.

By now, some have closed this book. They are not ready for the challenge. They are not ready to let go of their earthly identity.

However, if you're still reading, you are ready to move your life to the next level. You are ready to embrace your true identity and live your life in accordance with God's purpose.

Remember, there are no coincidences where God is concerned. Everything that happens in your life fits together as part of His perfect plan—including reading this book.

Jonah and His Really Big Fish

Do you feel like running away from this challenge? As if there has to be some mistake? God can't possibly expect you to answer His call, can He? If you feel that way, you're not alone!

If we impose our own interpretations on the small details, we likely do the same thing with the larger aspects as well.

Jonah felt the same way. In fact, when God called him to rise up and go, he fled from God, and in doing so fled from his call. Of course, we all know what happened next: Jonah got swallowed by a whale.

That's the image most of have seen in illustrated Bibles and biblical art—a huge whale swallowing little Jonah and giving him a ride in its belly until God caused the whale to spit him out. That's a great picture, isn't it? There's only one problem: The Bible never tells us it's a whale.

Jonah 1:17 clearly states, "Now the LORD had prepared a great fish to swallow up Jonah" (KJV). So why do we assume it was a whale? Because we, as humans, use our own experiences and mindsets to interpret Scripture, whether we know it or not.

Is the detail of the fish integral to the story? Probably not. But the point is, if we impose our own interpretations on the small details, we likely do the same thing with the larger aspects as well.

In order to grasp the depth and accuracy of God's Word, we have to let go of our old way of looking at things and be open to what God has in store.

Why do we do that? Perhaps we don't pay close enough attention to what we read. Maybe we have an image stuck in our heads from childhood that we are not willing to let go. Perhaps we think we already know what God wants to tell us, so we fill in the blanks with our own imaginations.

But in order to grasp the depth and accuracy of God's Word, we have to let go of our old way of looking at things and be open to what God has in store. This can be scary at times, but if we missed the detail about Jonah being swallowed by a large fish rather than a whale, what else might we be missing in the Bible?

My guess is: a lot.

For many of us, when we first encountered Jonah, it was presented as a lesson about disobedience and consequences. Jonah disobeyed God's command and, as a result, spent some unpleasant time in the belly of a whale. It's a valid lesson. When God tells us to do something, there is bound to be a very good reason, and when we disobey, the consequences aren't usually pleasant. But is there more? Can God pack more than one lesson into four short chapters? Of course He can!

It's a book about prayer. It's a story of deliverance. It's a tale of grace and justice, of rebellion and forgiveness, of arrogance and repentance.

At its core, Jonah is a story about our struggle with God and God's struggle with us. We don't like to admit it, but we all struggle with God. We fight Him. We argue with Him. We want His will to be *our* will sometimes, instead of the other way around. And God struggles right back, wrestling with our stubbornness, our self-righteousness, and our human nature.

That's why the Book of Jonah contains more depth than we may realize. It's a book about prayer. It's a story of deliverance. It's a tale of grace and justice, of rebellion and forgiveness, of arrogance and repentance. The story of Jonah represents the stages of our own growth as Christians and our journey to embracing our true identity in Christ.

From a technical point of view, some Bible scholars have pointed out that the Book of Jonah starts in an unusually abrupt way, with no background as to who Jonah is.

In light of this, there is some history to suggest that Jonah himself was already an established prophet. If that is true, the four chapters of Jonah would really be just a snapshot of one event in the man's life.

Why is that significant? Because it brings up an important point: Many of us have a preconceived notion of Jonah as the disobedient rebel—the man who defied God and tried to run away from His obligations.

We are being challenged, as we are every day, not to judge the man based upon this one incident.

We judge him on that basis, and because of that, are reluctant to be compared to him. It rubs against our grain when we hear that Jonah somehow embodies the struggle that we all endure, or the journey that we all face. We might picture Jonah as the bad guy in this, the one who deserved to face God's wrath and get swallowed by a sea creature.

But if this story is just a snapshot of one point in Jonah's life, then we have to consider that he was more than what we perceive him to be. He was God's prophet, who undoubtedly had good days and bad days and who did good things as well as bad things.

Again our perception is being challenged to see the bigger picture. We are being challenged to see the story as a lesson rather than as a condemnation of one man. We are being challenged, as we are every day, not to judge the man based upon this one incident, as we so often do.

If someone took a video of us on our worst day and then showed it to others, we would protest. We wouldn't want others to judge us based on that singular incident.

After all, did a full-grown man really get swallowed by some gigantic fish and live to tell about it?

So, yes, the Book of Jonah has yet another lesson to offer, one that teaches us not to judge others—or even ourselves—based upon a single snapshot, but always to strive to see the bigger picture, and to see the purpose and the person for whom they really are.

But It's Just a Story, Right?

Over the years, there has been some controversy and debate over whether the Book of Jonah is fact or fiction—whether it's meant to be taken literally or just as a metaphor or allegory. After all, did a full-grown man really get swallowed by some gigantic fish and live to tell about it? It seems far-fetched and outside of our normal realm of experience.

As a result, we write it off as allegory, saying that Jonah didn't *really* survive a huge fish swallowing him up. Non-believers like Thomas Paine, an American Revolutionary leader, have scoffed at the Book of Jonah as a childish joke. Paine wrote in *The Age of Reason* that the story of Jonah is a "fit story for ridicule, if it was written to be believed; or of laughter, if it was written to try what credulity could swallow; for, if it could swallow Jonah and the whale, it could swallow anything."[1]

Should we impose human limitations on God? The answer should be obvious.

But believers, too, are prone to categorize the Jonah narrative as being purely figurative. The historian and philosopher Russell Kirk respectfully, but misguidedly, labeled Jonah's story as primarily an "allegory" and "a symbol of the Jews' exile in Babylon," as well as "a tale of the marvelous" well suited for young readers.[2]

The Jonah story consists of multiple layers of meaning, to be sure, but many critics, commentators, and churchgoers, believer as well as non-believer, have alleged that it is merely symbolic. The same can be said for many other stories in the Bible: the Great Flood, the destruction of Sodom and Gomorrah, the plagues of Egypt, and the parting of the Red Sea.

How much of the Bible was made up, then?

Some people even try to explain away the miracles of Jesus. For instance, there is a certain sect of Christian scholars who teach that Jesus didn't really feed thousands of people with a few loaves of bread and a few fish. Rather, He inspired the crowd to share their meals with each other. These scholars deny that Jesus multiplied the food to feed the people since that would have been scientifically impossible by human standards. But isn't that the point?

When we try to squeeze God into a human box, we deny ourselves the opportunity to experience the supernatural in our lives.

Should we impose human limitations on God? The answer should be obvious. After all, our very lives are made supernatural through God's divinity. To relegate the story of Jonah to allegory would be to deny God's ability to perform miracles that transcend our understanding and experience.

When we try to squeeze God into a human box, we deny ourselves the opportunity to experience the supernatural in our lives. In short, we deny our true identity.

Think about it. To say that Jesus didn't perform miracles is to proclaim that the very fabric of the Christian faith—Jesus Christ rising from the dead—is nothing more than an allegorical story.

The Christian faith rests on the core understanding that God transcends the laws of nature, which He created. Without this basic principle, Christianity loses its meaning and we lose sight of our true identity.

In the story of Jonah, several miraculous events occur. Jonah 1:17 says, "Now the LORD had prepared a great fish to swallow up Jonah. And Jonah was in the belly of the fish three days and three nights" (KJV).

The Hebrew word translated as "prepare" literally means "to appoint." So, basically, God put into the mind of a fish to rise up and swallow Jonah whole the moment he was tossed into the sea. That alone is pretty amazing. As if that weren't enough, Jonah lived inside the fish for three days and three nights and then was spit out, unharmed. Another miracle.

Uncomfortable though they may be, challenges God puts in our paths are opportunities for growth.

That simple verse gives us two astounding bits of information about God's essence:

1. **His Supernatural Power:** God can alter the course of nature and cause supernatural events to occur to serve His great purpose.

2. **His Supernatural Protection:** Although God may place us in challenging or frightening circumstances, He also sees us through. God brought Jonah out of danger unscathed, and Jonah was wiser because of the experience.

Uncomfortable though they may be, challenges God puts in our paths are opportunities for growth. And through it all, He does not abandon us but, rather, uses His divine power to bring us through, changed for the better.

Of course, for most of us, the challenge won't be as dramatic as being gulped by a fish. But that doesn't mean our circumstances aren't daunting.

Our "fish" could be any number of frightening or challenging events—a job loss, a child on drugs, a divorce, the death of a loved one, a physical illness, and so on.

Yet whether we believe the crisis was appointed by God or not, we can trust that He will divinely bring us closer to our true identity as He carries us through unharmed.

Chapter One Questions

Question: How are you accepting and living out your identity in Christ? What more could you do in this regard?

_____

_____

_____

_____

_____

_____

_____

_____

_____

_____

Question: How are you living with intention and purpose? How is your church acting as the body of Christ? What more do you need to do?

_____

_____

_____

_____

_____

_____

_____

_____

_____

_____

_____

_____

Question: How do you tend to impose limitations on God? What is one way you tend to interpret Scripture according to your own experience, not God's Word?

_____

_____

_____

_____

_____

_____

_____

_____

_____

_____

Action: We are intended to be the body of Christ, physically and spiritually. But shifting our perspective and allowing ourselves to take on our true identity as the body of Christ means we have to do things that please God, not ourselves. In order to grasp the depth and accuracy of God's Word, we have to let go of our old way of looking at things and be open to what God has in store. For instance, we are being challenged every day not to judge a man based upon one incident. The Christian faith rests on the core understanding that God transcends the laws of nature, which He created. And whether we believe that a particular crisis was appointed by God or not, we can trust that He will divinely bring us closer to our true identity as He carries us through unharmed.

Chapter One Notes

CHAPTER TWO

Your Vocational Calling

Now the word of the LORD came unto Jonah the son of Amittai, saying, "Arise, go to Nineveh, that great city, and cry against it; for their wickedness is come up before me."

— Jonah 1:1–2 KJV

What does it mean to live out your calling? Some might say a person's "calling" is his or her vocation. Fair enough. But that begs the question: What is a vocation? Is it your job? The career you choose? How you spend your time? Or is it something more?

In some ways, "vocation" and "calling" are synonymous and are often used together. For instance, in Christianity, the phrase "vocational calling" is often used to refer to God's general call to mankind to become His children and accept His son, Jesus Christ, as Lord and Savior. It is God's invitation to become a part of His family and to live as a member of that family.

There is, however, a deeper meaning. It is a call to a way of life—a commitment that will serve as your center, no matter what you do.

If you are a believer, there will come a time when God will clarify the role you are to play in His divine and perfect plan.

It is not necessarily how you earn a living, but rather a *divine call* to pursue a God-directed lifestyle.

For instance, someone may have a call to preach. However, the person does not earn money preaching, so he or she waits tables at a local restaurant in order to make ends meet. Waiting tables is not that person's calling—preaching the gospel is.

When a person receives this deeper, divine calling, there are two aspects or subcategories:

1. A call to vocational identity
2. A call to vocational responsibility

Vocational Identity

There comes a time in every believer's life when God clarifies his or her purpose. This clarification may come later, or it may come sooner. It may be obvious, or it may be more obscure.

Nonetheless, if you are a believer, there will come a time when God will clarify the role you are to play in

His divine and perfect plan. This clarification defines your identity in relationship to your call.

The Book of Jeremiah states, "The word of the LORD came to me, saying, 'Before I formed you in the womb I knew you, before you were born I set you apart; I appointed you as a prophet to the nations'" (Jeremiah 1:4–6 NIV).

Sometimes vocational identity must be sought after through prayer, through fasting, and through persistence in one's faith.

God didn't just give Jeremiah His function; He anointed him with his vocational identity. It was not just a one-time action that God asked Jeremiah to perform. Rather, He called him to a way of life that defined who he was. It was woven into the fabric of his being, preordained and destined. In fact, his success in his calling as a prophet stemmed from the fact that it was his God-ordained nature.

It is that way with all of us. As believers, each and every one of us has a vocational identity that will be revealed by God at exactly the right time. No exceptions.

Sometimes vocational identity must be sought after through prayer, through fasting, and through persistence in one's faith. Make no mistake, though—God creates your vocational identity for you. It is not determined by your own judgment or circumstances. As with Jeremiah, it is an appointment by God.

Vocational Responsibility

Vocational responsibility encompasses the actions you take as a result of the vocational identity that God gives you.

Sleeping in a garage doesn't make you a car, right?

Your actions stem from an expression of your identity. So, if a person is called to be preacher, his vocational identity is that of a preacher. It is woven into his nature. His actions will then reflect that nature; he will preach the Word of God to an empty chair if he has to, but preaching God's Word will be his focus in life. It is his vocational responsibility.

Understanding the relationship between vocational identity and vocational responsibility is key to living a successful, fulfilling life for a believer.

Only God can assign your vocational identity. You may want to be a prophet, but if God has given you the role of preacher, and not that of prophet, then you will not be able to prophesize successfully, no matter how hard you try. If God has given you the role of preacher, and you go about trying to heal people instead, you are going to become very frustrated indeed because healing is not part of your vocational responsibility.

Sleeping in a garage doesn't make you a car, right? In the same way, you can't decide your own vocational identity. Trying to do so will only lead to heartache and trouble.

Oftentimes, staying true to your vocational identity involves tears and prayers and internal struggle.

It will always frustrate you to undertake a vocational responsibility outside of your true vocational identity. But what happens if a person, a believer, tries to deny his or her vocational responsibilities?

Let's go back to the Book of Jonah. God earmarked Jonah as a prophet. It was Jonah's vocational identity. This is made clear in the Second Book of Kings, where the text reads, "He restored the territory of Israel from the entrance of Hamath to the sea of Arabah according to the LORD God of Israel, which He had spoken through His servant Jonah, the son of Amittai, the prophet who was from Gath Hepher" (2 Kings 14:25 NKJV).

Historically, this prophecy took place prior to Jonah's call to go to Nineveh. This confirms that Jonah already had his vocational identity as a prophet. It isn't always easy to adhere to your vocational identity, and sometimes it's even harder to follow through with your vocational responsibilities.

Oftentimes, staying true to your vocational identity involves tears and prayers and internal struggle. It's the part no one sees—the personal conflict between your own expectations and God's.

Even after you're secure in the knowledge of your vocational identity, you may still struggle with undertaking the responsibilities He has given you in accordance with that identity.

Sometimes the scope of vocational responsibilities scares people. They feel that it's beyond what they can handle. And they may be right.

That's because your vocational responsibility sometimes involves doing things you don't want to do, or forfeiting things you really do want to do. Still, the fact remains that whenever you try to undertake tasks that are outside the scope of your vocational responsibilities, you will be met with frustration and disappointment.

Sometimes the scope of vocational responsibilities scares people. They feel that it's beyond what they can handle. And they may be right. They themselves could not handle it. That's why they need to stay connected to God through His Holy Spirit.

When God appoints your vocational identity, He also gives you the gifts and grace necessary to perform your vocational responsibilities. That is the miracle each and every believer experiences.

We are not left to flounder and figure out on our own how to do what God has called us to do. Instead, God not only gives us guidance, but He also gives us a full toolbox with everything we need to know to perform the tasks He has given us.

How effective would it be if someone with no musical talent, who couldn't even carry a tune, tried to lead worship?

For instance, if someone is given the vocational calling as worship leader, then God will give him the musical talent necessary to perform his vocational responsibilities successfully.

If God has called someone to be a preacher, then God will give him the ability to communicate the Word of God effectively to others. If God has called someone to be a prophet, then God will give that person the insight, foresight, and courage to carry on the tasks necessitated by those vocational responsibilities.

You get the idea. After all, how effective would it be if someone with no musical talent, who couldn't even carry a tune, tried to lead worship? The point is, if God calls, He also equips.

The Where and the Why

Up to this point, we've been speaking in terms of church-driven vocational callings, such as preacher or worship leader. But make no mistake: Vocational callings extend beyond the four walls of a church. Vocational identities encompass all types of jobs (e.g., doctors, salesmen, entrepreneurs, teachers). All of these callings can be God-appointed identities with God-driven responsibilities.

Whether you are called to stay, or to go temporarily, or to go permanently, that divine call comes from God.

And this brings up another point: When God gives someone a vocational calling, He doesn't necessarily keep that person in one place all the time. You may have a "home base," so to speak—a church or a community of believers to which you belong—but your vocational responsibilities may extend beyond that comfort sphere.

Just as Jonah was called away from his home base in Israel to preach in Nineveh, so too may our vocational responsibilities extend to places and circumstances that are far from home, either in a geographical sense or an emotional sense.

We may have our home base to return to, but it may only be a matter of time before we are challenged to go beyond the four walls of our community to fulfill our vocational responsibilities. Keep in mind, though, that the departure from our place of comfort may also be permanent. God may ask us to relinquish our ties to our community in order to fulfill our divine call. The common denominator in both scenarios, however, is that whether you are called to stay, or to go temporarily, or to go permanently, that divine call comes from God.

You can keep beating against the door, but if you are trying to go to a place where God doesn't want you to be, that door is going to remain closed.

This, of course, brings up the inevitable question: *How do I know? How do I know if the call is coming from God or from my own desires, wishes, and wants?*

We are given a clue in Paul's first letter to the Corinthians. Paul wrote, "But I will tarry here in Ephesus until Pentecost. For a great and effective door has been opened to me…" (1 Corinthians 16:8–9 NKJV).

Basically, then, if you are doing what God wants you to do, and you are doing it where God wants you to be, He will open great doors for you. Things will seem to click into place, sometimes in a way that defies human understanding.

The opposite is also true. If you are trying to undertake your vocational responsibilities in a place where you believe God intended you to be, yet you keep running into unexplainable resistance, it is a pretty good indicator that perhaps you are going in the wrong direction. Roadblocks and obstacles will come even when you are in the center of where God would have you. However, you will know that you are in the place God would have you, because you will sense His presence as you face these roadblocks and obstacles.

You can keep beating against the door, but if you are trying to go to a place where God doesn't want you to be, that door is going to remain closed. The Bible says that your gifts will make room for you. God will make a way for you. Roadblocks and closed doors are generally a sign that you have strayed off the path for which God anointed you and are taking matters into your own hands.

It's not about you—it's about Him. God has designed you for a purpose.

When God appoints your vocational identity and assigns your vocational responsibilities, He not only gives you the tools and abilities necessary to carry out your calling, but He also prepares the way for you.

Let's say God has called you to open a restaurant. Then He will give you the skills needed to cook wonderful meals, and He will ensure that you have customers come through your door.

Maybe God has ordained you to be the pastor of a church. If so, He will give you the ability to teach, lead, and inspire others. He will point you to the community that needs you most, and He will provide a congregation to shepherd.

God wants you to be successful at the vocational calling He has appointed for you because it all works to His great glory. You see, it's not about you—it's about Him. God has designed you for a purpose.

Stop wasting energy tugging on all of those locked doors. Instead, find the one that God is holding open just for you. When you do, you'll realize that by responding to your vocational calling, not only will you bring Him glory, but you will also experience true joy and fulfillment. That is the miraculous design He intended.

You Want Me to Go *Where*?

The idea of following God's vocational call and allowing Him to open doors for you may sound easy. After all, why wouldn't you let God usher a season of success into your life? Why wouldn't you go where He wants you to go if He is paving your way?

The point is, it doesn't matter how godly you are; following God's vocational call is bound to have its rough patches.

The fact is, there will likely be times when God asks you to go places you don't want to go—to serve people you don't really want to serve.

In the story of Jonah, God asked Jonah go to Nineveh. He called it a "great city." In order to understand the implications of this, we need to understand a little more about Jonah's background.

Jonah was an Israelite through and through. He didn't think too highly of the people of Nineveh. In fact, he didn't think of them as significant at all.

So, when God commanded him to go preach in Nineveh, Jonah was almost insulted by the idea. He was being asked to go to a city he disdained and preach to people he didn't hold in high regard. This is where the conflict came in. This is why he tried to flee from His vocational calling.

Just as with Jonah, God may purposefully put you in a situation that is specifically designed to challenge you.

The point is that it doesn't matter how godly you are; following God's vocational call is bound to have its rough patches. We may be asked to do what we consider below us or to serve people we don't see as significant.

But God sees them as significant. Just as with Jonah, God may purposefully put you in a situation that is specifically designed to challenge you. You might ask

God, "Why are You making it so tough on me? I'm trying to do what You want, but You're making it so difficult!"

Jonah most certainly had that same question. Is it because God has a strange sense of humor? Perhaps. But more likely it's because He wants you to grow—to move past your own selfishness and self-righteousness and start seeing things from *His* perspective.

If you're a parent, you're probably already familiar with this concept. Young children are often selfish in their actions. The world revolves around them and their happiness. If a young child has a favorite toy, how likely is he or she to share it, especially with a toddler whom the child doesn't like?

We, as parents, generally force our children to share, even with a child whom they don't necessarily like. Why? To teach them the value of generosity and the value of acceptance—of respecting and caring for others.

We see the world through tainted eyes. Our vision is clouded by our own limited perception and our own spiritual immaturity.

Our children may not like the idea—they may cry, whine, or throw a tantrum—but we do it anyway because we know it will help them grow as people. If we, with our flawed human nature, know enough to teach our children in this way, why wouldn't we expect the same from God, the perfect Father?

As noted earlier, our judgment is flawed. Our perspectives can be skewed. Remember how we found ourselves judging Jonah based on one snapshot of his life? How we saw a whale where God intended us to see a fish? We see the world through tainted eyes. Our vision is clouded by our own limited perception and our own spiritual immaturity. The cure? Spiritual growth. And as we discussed in chapter one, spiritual growth is usually uncomfortable, even painful.

Still, in order to achieve the fullness of our identity in Christ, it is necessary. That's why God challenges us. If it were always easy, we would never grow.

Jesus did not think of Himself when He gave His life for our sake. He could have called thousands of angels to come forth and save Him. But if He had, He would have been yielding to His own desires, not to the will of God.

Anyone who is familiar with the agony that Jesus endured in the Garden of Gethsemane knows that He faced a painful, difficult choice. But He chose to follow God's will because He knew it wasn't about Him; it was about God and His great glory. That is the level of obedience we must endeavor to achieve. That is the identity that we are called to embrace.

Chapter Two Questions

Question: Has God clarified your purpose in life? What is your understanding of your vocational identity?

_____
_____
_____
_____
_____
_____
_____
_____
_____
_____
_____

Question: Do you take vocational responsibility for the identity that God has given you? When have you tried doing something outside of your identity and felt frustrated or as if it wasn't where you were supposed to be?

_____
_____
_____
_____
_____

_____

_____

_____

_____

_____

_____

Question: When have you had to serve people you didn't like or in a place where you didn't want to be? How was that experience? After you finished serving, how did you feel? Or did you avoid the experience completely?

_____

_____

_____

_____

_____

_____

_____

_____

_____

Action: If you are a believer, there will come a time when God will clarify the role you are to play in His divine and perfect plan. As believers, each and every one of us has a vocational identity that will be revealed by God at exactly the right time. Vocational responsibility encompasses the actions you take as a result of the vocational identity that God gives you. Oftentimes, staying true to your vocational identity involves tears and prayers and internal struggle.

God not only gives us guidance, but He also gives us a full toolbox with everything we need to know to perform the tasks He has given us. When God appoints your vocational identity and assigns your vocational responsibilities, He gives you the tools and abilities necessary to carry out your calling, and He prepares the way for you. There will likely be times when God asks you to go places you don't want to go—to serve people you don't really want to serve. However, in order to achieve the fullness of our identity in Christ, obedience to His plan is necessary.

Chapter Two Notes

CHAPTER THREE

Roadblocks to the Miraculous

But Jonah rose up to flee unto Tarshish from the presence of the LORD, and went down to Joppa; and he found a ship going to Tarshish: so he paid the fare thereof, and went down into it, to go with them unto Tarshish from the presence of the Lord. But the LORD sent out a great wind into the sea, and there was a mighty tempest in the sea, so that the ship was like to be broken.

— Jonah 1:3–4 KJV

Sometimes we wonder why we don't see God moving in our lives. There are things we ask for, but He just doesn't come through. Even when we're not praying for anything specific, it can feel like He is not showing up in our lives.

Nothing terrible is happening, but nothing miraculous is happening, either. We don't have that sense of fulfillment and joy. Our lives are humdrum at best.

Is that what God intended? A humdrum existence? Of course not! God has called us to extraordinary lives, filled with the divine and supernatural. If that's the case, though, why do so many of us feel relegated to the ordinary? Why do so many of us settle for the mundane? Why do so many of us struggle with lives filled with frustration? It's because of the roadblocks we impose upon ourselves.

Nineveh may not be around anymore, but the type of people Jonah was reluctant to visit are still with us, aren't they?

You Say "Yes," I Say "No"

In the passage quoted at the beginning of this chapter, we see Jonah's reaction to the assignment God gives him. He didn't feel it was a great or important city, as God did. He didn't like the people because of their arrogance.

- They were condescending.

- They wouldn't listen to him.

- They wouldn't accept him.

- They wouldn't want his help (or anybody's help).

- They thought they had everything under control.

- He knew he wouldn't be appreciated. (In fact, he would most likely be scoffed at, scorned, and belittled.)

Nineveh may not be around anymore, but the type of people Jonah was reluctant to visit are still with us, aren't they? The people who believe they have everything under control. The people who don't need your help and don't want your interference. Most of us, at some point, come face-to-face with our own Nineveh.

Now, before you become too critical of Jonah, consider for a moment that he might have been more like you and me than we care to admit.

So how did Jonah respond to God's call to go to Nineveh? He responded with disobedience. He decided to make his own way and head out on a boat to Tarshish.

Not only was Tarshish in the opposite direction from Nineveh, but it was opposite in other ways as well. It was, in Jonah's estimation, more cultured, more refined, and more welcoming to him as an Israelite.

Jonah, using his own logic and reasoning, convinced himself that it would be a more suitable place for him to go—more comfortable and more accepting. He came to this decision on his own, snubbing the direction from his sovereign God, whom he had trusted so many times before.

Now, before you become too critical of Jonah, consider for a moment that he might have been more like you and me than we care to admit. His response was certainly not unique among humankind.

As was the case with Jonah's, our disobedience may seem like a good idea at the time. In fact, it might even be done with the best of intentions.

Can you think of a time when you were disobedient to God? Where you felt that your idea of how to handle a "Nineveh" situation was somehow better than God's way?

If you are like me, there are too many to count. In fact, there is only one person in all of history I can think of who was never disobedient to God's call. His name is Jesus. It's a fair bet that the rest of us haven't achieved that kind of perfection yet.

People who are called by God and serve God in numerous ways are still just people, and they will at times disobey. Whatever our vocational calling is, we still have a sinful nature.

As was the case with Jonah's, our disobedience may seem like a good idea at the time. In fact, it might even be done with the best of intentions. Still, it sets up a roadblock to God's blessings.

If we claim to have a divine call in our lives, we have to be prepared to accept the consequences. By acknowledging our divine call, we acknowledge that God has the final say in where we are led and what we are called to do. As believers, we hold to a faith that puts God's way before our own.

Make no mistake. Disobedience is sin, and sin always separates us from God.

Our God is good and righteous and will not lead us astray. If He calls us, He will also equip us. By accepting our vocational calling, we give ourselves over to God in complete trust.

But sometimes, when we are asked to do something particularly difficult or challenging, our trust wavers. Doubt creeps in. Our egos get in the way. Indignation, rationalization, and justification sneak in, too.

We start asking ourselves dangerous "what if" questions: What if God is wrong this time? What if I didn't hear Him correctly? What if this is not really what I'm supposed to be doing? What if I made a mistake? What if it doesn't go the way it's supposed to go? These doubts erode our trust and inevitably lead us down a road to disobedience.

How Much Does Disobedience Cost?

Make no mistake. Disobedience is sin, and sin always separates us from God. No, it doesn't mean we stop living our vocational call, but it does slow down the process of reclaiming our true identity. It prevents us from experiencing the supernatural in our lives.

Even when we are disobedient, God does not turn from us. He continues to call us back to do what He wants us to do—that which will bring Him the greatest glory.

You see, Jonah did not run from his vocational calling. Rather, he ran from his vocational responsibility. In other words, he ran from what he was called to do, but he still retained his vocational identity as God's prophet.

The same is true with us. Even when we are disobedient, God does not turn from us. We still retain our vocational identity. He continues to call us back to do what He wants us to do—that which will bring Him the greatest glory. And that which will bring us the greatest fulfillment.

That doesn't mean disobedience comes without a price, though. Sin and disobedience always cost you, usually in more ways than one. For instance, Jonah had to pay a fare to get on board the boat to Tarshish. The Bible doesn't tell us how much, but I would venture to guess it wasn't cheap. Then, after he paid a hefty fare, he never even made it to his destination. So Jonah paid for his disobedience, and it got him nowhere.

The price we pay for disobedience may not be a monetary toll, but it will most definitely be an emotional toll. Oftentimes, we can see the miraculous just on the horizon, but it's always just out of reach.

Most of us have had an experience in which something seems so desirable that we yield to that desire, even though we know, deep down, it is disobedience to God's will and calling.

God's favor is freely given. The only cost to us is obedience to His will.

At first, giving into desire seems satisfying, but that satisfaction is short-lived. Then guilt sets in, or disappointment or disillusionment. We don't feel joyful. We don't feel blessed. We feel empty. Something is missing—and that something is God's supernatural blessing. It's the joy and fulfillment that we can only achieve by following God's vocational calling in our lives—by yielding in obedience to the challenges He places before us rather than taking the easy way out.

God's favor is freely given. The only cost to us is obedience to His will. We cannot receive His favor if we are disobedient to His will. The favor of God is often referred to as the face of God. Thus, if we turn from His face, we cannot know the joy that flows when He smiles upon us.

It is not God's doing. It's ours. We're the ones who turn from Him when we disobey. Sin has a hefty price tag and, in the end, gets us nowhere.

We can rationalize our actions and justify our motives. But the fact is, God's reasons will trump ours every time. His justifications are mightier than ours. His motives are worthier than ours.

His plan for our lives is bigger than anyone could imagine. He does not want His children to wallow in mediocrity.

He demands that we submit to His will, but He doesn't do this to disparage or deride us. Quite the opposite: He demands submission so that He can raise us up to levels we've never imagined.

His plan for our lives is bigger than anyone could imagine. He does not want His children to wallow in mediocrity. Instead, He wants to raise us up to our fullest potential. He wants us to reach the absolute joy that comes from fully realizing our true identity in Christ. Will the path be easy? No. It will be challenging, even painful. But it will be worth it.

And through it all, God will continue to equip and guide you, letting the joy and comfort of His presence fulfill you along the way.

Chapter Three Questions

Question: When have you disobeyed God by making a decision or taking a route in your life that you thought was best, instead of listening to God and His plan?

_____
_____
_____
_____
_____
_____
_____
_____
_____
_____

Question: What was the cost of your disobedience to God?

_____
_____
_____
_____
_____
_____

_____

_____

_____

_____

Question: How did God redirect you from disobedience back toward His plan for your life?

_____

_____

_____

_____

_____

_____

_____

_____

_____

_____

Action: People who are called by God and serve God in numerous ways are still just people, and they will at times disobey. But make no mistake: Disobedience is sin, and sin always separates us from God. As believers, we hold to a faith that puts God's way before our own. The price we pay for disobedience may not be a monetary toll, but it will most definitely be an emotional toll. Yet through it all, God will continue to equip and guide us, letting the joy and comfort of His presence fulfill us along the way.

Chapter Three Notes

CHAPTER FOUR

Accountability Counts

And you, my child, will be called a prophet of the Most High; for you will go on before the Lord to prepare the way for him, to give his people the knowledge of salvation through the forgiveness of their sins, because of the tender mercy of our God...

— Luke 1:76–78 NIV

In the verse above, Luke is telling us what Zechariah, the father of John the Baptist, said to John when John was just a child. Zechariah was speaking words given to him by God, confirming John's vocational calling as the great prophet who would prepare the way for the coming of Jesus Christ.

Facing Facts

As I mentioned in the previous chapter, the expression "the face of God" actually represents the favor of God. However, it also represents something else: accountability.

Specifically, it represents our accountability to God in performing the responsibilities of our vocational calling.

When Zechariah spoke those words to young John the Baptist, he was not only confirming the boy's vocational identity (a prophet of God), but also placing a yoke of responsibility on the child's shoulders.

If the boss is standing right behind us at work, we know he's watching our every move and we know he will hold us accountable.

Yes, John the Baptist was God's prophet, and nothing would change that. But along with that title came responsibility. He was charged with the task of preparing the way for Jesus Christ, telling people of His imminent coming, and preparing their hearts and minds through repentance and baptism to receive Him when He came.

Furthermore, John was to do this "through the tender mercy of God," or in other words, with God's face looking upon him. John the Baptist had God's full attention.

Having God's full attention upon you means that you have His assistance and guidance—His favor. But it also means that you have accountability.

For those of us with jobs, we tend to work a bit more diligently when the boss is looking over our shoulder, don't we? If the boss is standing right behind us at work, we know he's watching our every move and we know he will hold us accountable.

We want to impress him, to please him, to make sure we do the job right so that we get our paycheck—maybe even a raise. We pay greater attention to what we're supposed to be doing.

In most instances, disobedience is rooted in a desire to escape accountability—a decision to do things your own way without having to answer to anyone, not even to God.

When God issues a vocational calling, His face is upon us. He is standing over our shoulder, watching our every move. Along with that comes accountability.

God gave Jonah the task to go to Nineveh. Jonah was therefore accountable to God to perform that task. However, he didn't want to be accountable to God. He wanted to perform the duties of his vocational identity, but he wanted to do them in his own way.

So he fled not only from God's favor but also from His accountability. That desire to do things his own way was the root of his disobedience.

In fact, in most instances, disobedience is rooted in a desire to escape accountability—a decision to do things your own way without having to answer to anyone, not even to God. The problem is, a call without accountability is destined to fail.

So many of us never realize the fulfillment of God's call in our lives because of a deep-rooted rebellion that keeps us from accepting our accountability.

Can't Have One Without the Other

As we discussed earlier, a true vocational calling comes from God. That means that God shapes our vocational identity and our vocational responsibilities. In turn, that means we must remain obedient to God and remain accountable to Him by our actions. In order to pursue our vocational calling successfully and share in the supernatural miracles that await, we are bound by obedience and accountability.

So many of us never realize the fulfillment of God's call in our lives because of a deep-rooted rebellion that keeps us from accepting our accountability.

Many times, this rebellion is of a passive-aggressive nature, which means that on the surface we nod and agree with regard to our responsibilities. We know what they are. We know what God wants us to do, but in our hearts, we also know that we are not going to do those things.

For instance, suppose you're at work and your supervisor comes up to you and hands you an assignment. You understand what he or she wants you to do and you have all the tools needed to do it, so you nod and agree as you accept the assignment.

Then, as soon as your supervisor walks away, you tuck it under a pile of other work with no intention of ever actually performing the task he or she gave you. That is passive-aggressive rebellion. Your mouth says "yes," but your heart says "no." Your actions reflect what is in your heart.

God loves us too much to simply let us walk away from the extraordinary life He has planned for us.

People rebel in a passive-aggressive manner for various reasons. In our example, it may be that the employee doesn't have the nerve to stand up to the supervisor, or it may be that the employee wanted to win the approval of the supervisor by saying "yes."

It could be fear. It could be apathy. Whatever the reason, the outcome is still the same: The project will not get done. And there will be a price to pay. There always is. Running from accountability always brings consequences.

God loves us too much to simply let us walk away from the extraordinary life He has planned for us. When God gives you a vocational calling, He is giving you a life of meaning and destiny—a life filled with purpose and fulfillment and supernatural miracles.

Life lived without accountability is life steeped in mediocrity. It is a life of unfulfilled dreams and unrealized potential. Whether out of fear, stubbornness, laziness, or any one of a hundred other reasons, by running from accountability—by falling into the trap of disobedience—we cheat ourselves out of everything good that God has prepared for us.

God won't let us get far in our disobedience without reminding us of our responsibilities, our mission, and our destiny.

This is what happened to Jonah. He acted with a passive-aggressive nature. God told him to go to Nineveh. Jonah arose in the morning, but then he got on a boat going in the opposite direction.

Passive-aggressive rebellion.

Disobedience.

Running from accountability.

But, as God showed us in the example of Jonah, even when we rebel and turn away from His face, He won't turn away from us. He won't let us get far in our disobedience without reminding us of our responsibilities, our mission, and our destiny. He loves us too much to just let us slip away into a life of mediocrity. And if we persist in our rebelliousness, He will persist in His pursuit.

This is demonstrated very dramatically in Jonah's story while he was still on the boat. To turn Jonah away from his disobedience, God pursued him in three very clear ways: through a storm, a stranger, and exposure.

The Storm

Then the LORD sent a great wind on the sea, and such a violent storm arose that the ship threatened to break up.

— Jonah 1:4 NIV

Jonah boarded a boat to Tarshish, knowing full well that he was going against what God had commanded him to do. According to Scripture, after he boarded, he found a comfy spot below the deck and fell asleep.

In the meantime, a great storm arose, and a great wind stirred the sea. How bad was the storm? Scripture says, "All the sailors were afraid and each cried out to his own god" (Jonah 1:5 NIV).

It was not God's desire to hurt Jonah, but to get his attention and redirect him.

These men were sailors by profession, used to navigating the seas. And they were all frightened. Not just the inexperienced ones—all of them.

They were so scared that they each started praying to their own god. But this did little to get Jonah's attention, for the sailors found him asleep in the bottom of the boat.

There are two aspects to this part of the story that bear closer analysis: first, the storm; second, the boat itself. The storm was not meant to destroy Jonah. How do we know this? By the fact that the boat stayed in one piece. These experienced sailors thought the boat would break apart, but it didn't. It was not God's desire to hurt Jonah, but to get his attention and redirect him.

When troubles come, too many of us are so busy shouting about the devil's interference that we don't stop and pray for discernment.

We all face storms in our lives. Sometimes literally, as when we see the devastation brought by powerful weather events. And oftentimes figuratively, as when we face problems and difficulties of all types.

Many times, when we face storms in our lives, we are unclear if they are storms brought by God for a purpose or storms brought by our enemy, Satan. In the case of Jonah, the scripture clearly tells us that God brought the storm into his life. It was His doing. But what about for us? How do we know if a storm is God-driven or brought by the enemy?

It takes a degree of spiritual maturity to distinguish between the two.

When troubles come, too many of us are so busy shouting about the devil's interference that we don't stop and pray for discernment. When trouble comes into our lives, instead of sleeping like Jonah, we need to be awake and aware and ready to pray to God so that He can enlighten us as to the source and reason. When God brings storms into our lives, He does it to save us from ourselves and to redirect our footsteps. He brings trouble to shine a light on disobedience and set us back on the right path.

Are we truly pursuing the vocational call that God has laid on our hearts? Are we truly where we are supposed to be physically, emotionally, and spiritually?

On the other hand, when Satan interferes in our lives, it is with the intent to destroy, to kill, and to steal. When we are not sure, we need to stop and do an inventory of our lives.

What are we doing? Are we truly pursuing the vocational call that God has laid on our hearts? Are we truly where we are supposed to be physically, emotionally, and spiritually? We have to ask ourselves these honest questions and give ourselves honest answers.

In addition, though, we need to pray. We need to ask God to show us the real reason for the storm, and what we need to do in response to it.

Another aspect to consider in this verse is the boat. Jonah paid to get on that boat, and once aboard, everyone on it became his accomplices in disobedience. The boat was the instrument by which he tried to escape his accountability.

In turn, everyone was affected by the terrible storm emotionally, physically, spiritually, and relationally. The sailors became upset and very frightened as the waves and wind threatened to tear the ship to pieces.

When we rebel against God, we have our own "boat"—our own methods by which we try to escape accountability.

The sailors turned to their own gods in prayer, but to no avail. Finally, they figured out that Jonah's presence was the cause of their troubles, and they decided they had to take action against him.

When we rebel against God, we have our own "boat"—our own methods by which we try to escape accountability. We try to go to a place or situation that distracts us from our vocational responsibilities. And it doesn't have to be a physical location. It can be a job, a hobby, excessive Internet browsing—anything that takes us away from responsibilities that we are supposed to be pursuing.

As a result, the people and things with which we surround ourselves in our attempts to escape accountability will be affected by the consequences of our rebellion. On the flip side, they will all be affected positively when we turn back to our responsibilities.

The Stranger

> *But Jonah had gone below deck, where he lay down and fell into a deep sleep. The captain went to him and said, "How can you sleep? Get up and call on your god! Maybe he will take notice of us so that we will not perish."*

> *— Jonah 1:5-6 NIV*

Jonah had a rather odd reaction to the turmoil of the storm: He fell into a deep sleep. See what happened here? Professional seamen running around trying to keep the ship from sinking in this horrendous storm while the person who actually caused the storm was sound asleep in an area hidden away below the deck.

Sometimes we can sink so deeply into the lowest part of our nature that we are oblivious to the storm raging around us.

This small fact speaks volumes. It depicts how easily we can become comfortable with our own sins and bad habits. In fact, we may become so comfortable that we don't even realize the turmoil we are causing around us.

Jonah fell asleep in the lowest part of the ship, a statement that is both literal and figurative. Sometimes we can sink so deeply into the lowest part of our nature that we are oblivious to the storm raging around us.

Our eyes are closed, and we no longer see the problems resulting from our disobedience. We need someone to shake us awake and remind us of our accountability, as the captain did with Jonah.

The captain and Jonah were strangers to each other. Except for the fact that Jonah paid a fare to hitch a ride on his ship, the captain didn't really know him. Yet he was the one who came forth into Jonah's life and inspired him to take action.

God places people in our lives who jolt us back to reality, ask the tough questions, and give us that overdue wake-up call so that we see our circumstances from a clearer perspective.

Was the captain a priest? A fellow Israelite? A wise man or scholar? No! He was a sea captain and a pagan (remembering that, in the previous verse, he and the other sailors were calling upon "his own god"). He was most likely rough around the edges and probably not too happy with Jonah at that given moment.

He was an unlikely candidate, yet God used him to rouse Jonah from his sleep.

God places people like that in our lives as well—people who jolt us back to reality, ask the tough questions, and give us that overdue wake-up call so that we see our circumstances from a clearer perspective. They are not always the people we expect or appreciate. But if we listen, we can hear God speaking through them. It's never pleasant when someone points out our flaws or mistakes. However, this all goes back to what we said about growth. Growth usually involves some degree of discomfort and pain. The people who shock us, confront us, and maybe even insult us can help us see the roadblocks that we have placed in our own path and the storms that threaten to tear our security to pieces.

Have you ever found yourself in a situation in which others didn't take you seriously or treat you with any kind of deference?

Through the Captain's Eyes

Let's switch things around for a moment and look at the story from the captain's eyes. What kind of an impression was Jonah giving him? One of care, or of apathy?

Here was Jonah, a great prophet from the God of Abraham, anointed to fulfill an incredible vocational responsibility; but when trouble arose, what did he do? He went to sleep!

Should the captain have recognized him for who he was? Was Jonah's vocational identity readily apparent?

Of course not. What the captain saw was a sleeper, someone who, for whatever reason, had no concern about what was happening and preferred to hide from his responsibilities. His actions didn't match up with whom he claimed to be.

Have you ever found yourself in a situation in which others didn't take you seriously or treat you with any kind of deference? When others didn't seem at all impressed by the fact that you were appointed with a vocational calling?

If I go around telling everyone that I am on a strict health-food diet, but then proceed to eat five candy bars and three bowls of ice cream in their presence, how much credibility do I hold?

It could be because your actions have not been corresponding to the identity you proclaim. You might be talking the talk, but not walking the walk.

This is not a new concept. In his letter to the Ephesians, Paul implored the Ephesians to "walk in a manner worthy of the calling with which you have been called…" (Ephesians 4:1 NASB). He was beseeching them to walk the walk, not just talk the talk.

The old adage that "actions speak louder than words" holds a lot of truth. For instance, if I go around telling everyone that I am on a strict health-food diet, but then proceed to eat five candy bars and three bowls of ice cream in their presence, how much credibility do I hold? Our actions speak volumes about who we are.

Of course, we don't undertake our vocational responsibilities to please other people. We do it to please God. In fact, seeking the approval of others is often a losing battle. Some people won't be happy no matter what you do.

No matter what you do, you will never be able to please everybody, and some people will always find a reason to criticize.

Jesus himself recognized that fact. In Matthew 11:16–19, He states, "But to what shall I compare this generation? It is like children sitting in the market places, who call out to the other children, and say, 'We played the flute for you, and you did not dance; we sang a dirge, and you did not mourn.' For John came neither eating nor drinking, and they say, 'He has a demon!' The Son of Man came eating and drinking, and they say, 'Behold, a gluttonous man and a drunkard, a friend of tax collectors and sinners!' Yet wisdom is vindicated by her deeds" (NASB).

In other words, no matter what you do, you will never be able to please everybody, and some people will always find a reason to criticize. While the opinions of others may help us to adjust our perspective and gauge whether our actions are in line with our calling, the approval of others should not be our goal. The only approval we should seek is God's, and our goal through our actions should be to walk worthily and seek His favor.

Exposed!

Each man said to his mate, "Come, let us cast lots so we may learn on whose account this calamity has struck us." So they cast lots and the lot fell on Jonah. Then they said to him, "Tell us, now! On whose account has this calamity struck us? What is your occupation? And where do you come from? What is your country? From what people are you?"

— Jonah 1:7–8 NASB

When there is a heavy call on your life and you are in disobedience to that call, God will manufacture conditions that will expose you and your mess for what you are. Jonah tried to escape the consequences of his actions by crawling away to the lowest part of the ship and falling asleep.

God took notice. He wasn't going to let Jonah get away that easily. He manufactured a storm, complete with fierce wind and waves. He sent a stranger to give Jonah a wake-up call, literally and figuratively.

If we refuse to hold ourselves accountable for our actions or inactions, God will manufacture circumstances in our lives that will expose us and bring us to accountability.

Then, to top it off, He exposed Jonah's sin by creating a storm for the men on the ship to deal with. They drew lots to figure out who was responsible. God intervened, the lot fell on Jonah, and the men started asking him questions. Jonah was no longer some obscure figure hiding in the bottom of the boat. Now he was front and center, and his disobedience was exposed.

God didn't do this to embarrass or degrade Jonah. Rather, He did it to bring him back to accountability. In the same way, if we refuse to hold ourselves accountable for our actions or inactions, God will manufacture circumstances in our lives that will expose us and bring us to accountability.

As humans, we are very good at blaming. Adam blamed Eve, and Eve blamed the snake. Mankind is all about blame.

When there's trouble in the air, we tend to be good pretenders. We pretend everything is fine. We pretend not to notice the problems. And then, when we can no longer ignore them, we tend to point fingers.

As humans, we are very good at blaming. Take Adam and Eve for instance. Adam blamed Eve, and Eve blamed the snake. Mankind is all about blame.

But God is all about accountability. He won't let us play the blame game for very long. He will create inescapable circumstances that will inevitably reveal the truth to others. This can be harsh and painful, but it is a necessary pain, designed to bring us back into favor with God.

Looking at the next verse, though, it is clear that Jonah still hadn't given up the fight. Essentially, he had been called out for sleeping on the job and had been exposed as the cause of the calamity that had befallen the ship, but when the men asked him who he was, he answered, "I am a Hebrew and I worship the LORD, the God of heaven, who made the sea and the land" (Jonah 1:9 NIV).

As Christians, when it comes to accountability, a key question we must ask ourselves is not only "What have I done?" but also "What am I doing?"

While this was a true statement, it's the information that Jonah left *out* that is significant. He did not say that he was a prophet from God. He only identified himself by nationality, perhaps hoping that it would carry some weight and get him off the hook.

But the men didn't let up on their questioning. In fact, the statement incriminated him further, and they asked the deeper question: "What have you done?" (Jonah 1:10 NIV).

And if that weren't enough, they followed up by asking him what they needed to do to him to end the storm (Jonah 1:11). Not only had the men called him back to accountability, but they also called him to act upon that accountability—to fix the situation that he had caused. These were some tough demands.

As Christians, when it comes to accountability, a key question we must ask ourselves is not only "What have I done?" but also "What am I doing?" These questions require honest introspection and soul-searching.

Are we holding ourselves accountable in our walk with God, or are we too busy playing the blame game? Do our actions reflect our vocational identity, or are we asleep to our own disobedience? Are we hiding behind a fabricated persona?

Honest answers to these questions will reveal your true identity and the fulfillment of your vocational calling.

WORKBOOK

Chapter Four Questions

Question: How do you hold yourself accountable and make sure your actions correspond to your identity in Christ?

_____

_____

_____

_____

_____

_____

_____

_____

_____

_____

Question: Who helps hold you accountable? How?

_____

_____

_____

_____

_____

_____

_____

_____

_____

_____

Question: What "boat" have you used to try to escape accountability in the past? How did you move past your reliance on this means of avoidance—or do you still try to use it?

_____

_____

_____

_____

_____

_____

_____

_____

_____

_____

Action: Having God's full attention upon you means that you have His assistance and guidance—His favor. In order to pursue our vocational calling successfully, and share in the supernatural miracles that await, we are bound by obedience and accountability.

When God gives you a vocational calling, He is giving you a life of meaning and destiny—a life filled with purpose and fulfillment and miracles. Accordingly, He brings trouble to shine a light on disobedience and set us back on the right path. We need someone to shake us awake and remind us of our accountability, as the captain did with Jonah.

As Christians, when it comes to accountability, a key question we must ask ourselves is not only, "What have I done?" but also, "What am I doing?" These questions require honest introspection and soul-searching.

Chapter Four Notes

CHAPTER FIVE

Our Bond with God

So they said to him, "What should we do to you that the sea may become calm for us?"—for the sea was becoming increasingly stormy. He said to them, "Pick me up and throw me into the sea. Then the sea will become calm for you, for I know that on account of me this great storm has come upon you."

— *Jonah 1:11–12 NASB*

Does it ever seem as if God asks us to do the impossible? Does it ever feel that what He wants from you makes no sense? And no matter how many times you trace the maze with your finger, there is no logical way out? Think back to the earlier chapter when we considered the idea of miracles. By their very definition, miracles are occurrences that defy logic and flout the laws of nature. They are supernatural, which means they go beyond the natural laws we know.

So, if God calls us to a supernatural destiny, what makes us think that our challenges would appear logical? What makes us think that they would make sense?

Our vocational identity and our vocational responsibilities transcend and defy the laws of nature. That's why God wants us to put our trust in Him and obey Him without reservation.

We need God's favor in order to accomplish our vocational responsibilities. But when we are disobedient, we turn from the face of God.

You're Not in This Alone

God doesn't expect us to undertake our vocational responsibilities by ourselves. Rather, He wants us to rely on His strength and wisdom. If we believe that God appointed us a task but we don't need Him to accomplish it, then it's probably not from Him.

We need God's favor in order to accomplish our vocational responsibilities. But when we are disobedient, we turn from the face of God.

Still, it is important to note that even when our fellowship with God is fractured, we remain in union with Him. We are still connected with Him through the Holy Spirit. God promised us that He will never leave us, even when we turn from Him, and God is not one to break promises. But we can hinder fellowship with Him through our sin and disobedience.

To illustrate the difference, consider the situation when your own child disobeys you. Perhaps you send him to his room, or take away his computer privileges or cell phone.

The fellowship between the two of you is broken for the time being. Your child is not receiving the benefits of your favor (aka computer or cell phone use). Yet he is still your child. You are still there for him. The love still exists between the two of you.

We must come to Him with an attitude of total surrender, ready to yield our will to His.

What happens when our fellowship with God is broken? Obviously, we cannot move forward in our vocational call without His help. So what do we do to repair that relationship?

We must come to Him with an attitude of total surrender, ready to yield our will to His. Some scholars have postulated that Jonah was in such a deep sleep in the boat because he was depressed by his disobedience. Others believe it was because he was exhausted by the emotional turmoil. Either way, God is not impressed or motivated by such things.

If Jonah was depressed, he brought it on himself. If he was exhausted, it was his own doing. The only way to escape such a situation is by turning to God in surrender, not by wallowing in self-pity.

The Ultimate Surrender

Once Jonah's disobedience was exposed, he finally relented. The men asked him what to do to calm the storm, and he basically told him they needed to throw him overboard. This was a gutsy move on his part.

There is one certainty that we can hold on to—God will not let us go. He will carry us through the storm.

The sea was in an uproar, and being thrown into it meant certain death. He was willing, at that point, to die for the sake of accountability. He was ready to give his life over for these men whom he'd put in jeopardy because of his disobedience.

For most of us, in order for the storms in our own lives to stop, we need to surrender completely to God. We need to die to ourselves and submit completely to God's call on our life.

It's a scary proposition. There are a lot of uncertainties involved. Still, there is one certainty that we can hold on to—God will not let us go. He will carry us through the storm.

Consider the sailors who were on the boat with Jonah. When the storm initially began, they tried throwing cargo overboard, hoping it would help them endure the storm. Not one of them thought to throw himself into the sea, though. They were willing to get rid of excess baggage but not surrender their own lives.

And the storm continued.

It is that way with us, a lot of times. We give God half measures. We give Him *some* of our lives but certainly not all. That's too risky. And so our storms continue.

Interference with the Plan

Jonah told the sailors to pick him up and throw him into the sea. But that's not what they did—at least not at first. Instead, they did their best to row back to land. But they could not, for the sea grew even wilder than before (Jonah 1:13).

Do you have people in your life who, even with the best of intentions, try to stop you from pursuing your vocational responsibilities?

Why didn't they just listen to Jonah right away? Most likely, they didn't want to be responsible for his death. Whether it was out of compassion, fear, or guilt, they knew that Jonah couldn't possibly survive if they threw him overboard. They were trying to save him from himself.

Do you have people like that in your life? People who, even with the best of intentions, try to stop you from pursuing your vocational responsibilities? Many times, these people are the ones closest to you—the ones who have the most influence.

Consider the relationship between Jesus and Peter. They were close. Peter could be considered His right-hand man. But what happened? Peter tried to convince Jesus not to go through with His destiny. After Jesus explained to His disciples what He must endure in order to bring salvation, "Peter took him aside and began to rebuke him. 'Never, Lord!' he said. 'This shall never happen to you!'" (Matthew 16:22 NIV).

> *Jesus was not likening Peter to Satan, but rather telling him, in no uncertain terms, that his attempts to thwart the will of God were born of his own weakness and sinful nature.*

Did Peter say this to be mean or manipulative? No. He said it out of genuine concern, worry, and the desire to not see Jesus suffer. He didn't want to lose Him.

Jesus responded by saying, "Get behind me, Satan! You are a stumbling block to me; you do not have in mind the things of God, but merely human concerns" (Matthew 16:23 NIV).

At that moment, Jesus recognized Peter as a roadblock to His vocational calling. Jesus was not likening Peter to Satan, but rather telling him, in no uncertain terms, that his attempts to thwart the will of God were born of his own weakness and sinful nature—

that while his intentions were good, he was not considering the will of God, but rather his own desires and expectations.

Great Expectations

We all have expectations about our lives. When we're children, we dream of all the paths we could take. However, when we surrender our lives to God, there is a radical shift.

Some people won't like this. Some might even be angry. They will try to return you to your old way of doing things.

This change is bound to affect other people. You don't do the things you did before. You don't go to the same places or spend your time pursuing your old interests.

Some people won't like this. Some might even be angry. They will try to return you to your old way of doing things. There will be "Peters" in your life who will try to sway you from your vocational calling.

So what do we do? Sometimes, as with Jonah, separation is necessary—a physical parting of ways. Jonah physically separated himself from the men who were trying to row to shore.

Other times, God will intervene and stop those who are interfering. In Jonah's story, when the men tried to row back to shore, God increased the tempest, making it impossible and basically forcing them to change their minds.

The point is, if we surrender to God, we put Him in control. We don't relinquish that control to others.

When God is telling us to do something that conflicts with what others want us to do, our default course of action should be to trust Him alone.

Many times, the place where God wants you to go involves letting go of that which is secure and comfortable in order to embrace the unknown.

Uncharted Waters

Going with God usually means going into the unknown. Jonah couldn't see what lay below the surface of the water, but he wanted to be thrown in there anyway.

At that point, he had surrendered his will to God's and knew that, whatever happened, He would be with him despite his earlier disobedience. He relinquished his comfortable sleeping spot in the bottom of the boat to go forth into the unknown and the frightening.

Does that sound familiar? Many times, the place where God wants you to go involves letting go of that which is secure and comfortable in order to embrace the unknown. But unless you are willing to do that, you cannot move forward into your supernatural destiny.

You have to be willing to dive into uncharted waters.

WORKBOOK

Chapter Five Questions

Question: In what ways have you submitted your life to God? What results are you experiencing?

_____

_____

_____

_____

_____

_____

_____

_____

_____

_____

_____

Question: In what areas of your life are you holding out against complete surrender to God? What things are you trying to do on your own? How is that going for you?

_____

_____

_____

_____

_____

_____

_____

_____

_____

_____

_____

Question: In what aspects of your life is God telling you to leave your comfort zone? What will your first step be toward a fuller surrender to God's design for your life?

_____

_____

_____

_____

_____

_____

_____

_____

_____

_____

Action: If we believe that God has appointed us a task, but we don't need Him to accomplish it, then it's probably not from Him. We need to die to ourselves and submit completely to God's call on our life. When God is telling us to do something that conflicts with what others want us to do, our default course of action should be to trust Him alone. Many times, the place where God wants you to go involves letting go of that which is secure and comfortable in order to embrace the unknown. But unless you are willing to do that, you cannot move forward into your supernatural destiny.

Chapter Five Notes

_____

_____

_____

_____

_____

_____

_____

_____

_____

_____

_____

_____

_____

_____

_____

_____

_____

_____

_____

_____

_____

_____

_____

_____

_____

_____

CHAPTER SIX

The Sovereignty of God

Then they cried out to the LORD, "Please, LORD, do not let us die for taking this man's life. Do not hold us accountable for killing an innocent man, for you, LORD, have done as you pleased." Then they took Jonah and threw him overboard, and the raging sea grew calm. At this, the men greatly feared the LORD, and they offered a sacrifice to the LORD and made vows to him.

— Jonah 1:14–16 NIV

Isn't it amazing what God can do with a situation we consider impossible? After the sailors on the boat tried to save Jonah—to fix the situation by rowing back to shore—they finally gave up and threw him overboard, certain that it would result in his death. In so doing, though, they were confronted with the sovereignty of the one true God. They recognized that, regardless of their actions, the Lord of Jonah had done as He pleased.

You see, most of the pagan gods of Jonah's time could often be controlled or manipulated by the actions of men. Jonah's God could not. They declared Jonah's

God as sovereign above all others, and they offered sacrifices and praise to Him.

God does what He wants to do, when He wants to do it. Why? Because it pleases Him.

They were, in other words, converted. Even while Jonah was in rebellion, God used him to bring others to Christ. Had Jonah never gotten on that boat, those men would have gone about their daily lives, worshipping their pagan gods and never being faced with the sovereignty of the one true God.

God is God and We Are Not

Sometimes God puts storms in our lives because He wants us to recognize and acknowledge His sovereignty. He wants us truly to come to terms with the fact that He is in control. Always.

God does what He wants to do, when He wants to do it. Why? Because it pleases Him. He gives gifts to whomever He chooses, He reaps and sows as He pleases, He builds and destroys as He sees fit, and He blesses and curses as He wants.

As Paul stated in his letter to the Romans, "For He says to Moses, 'I will have mercy on whom I have mercy and I will have compassion on whom I have compassion.' So then it depends not on human will or exertion, but on God, who has mercy" (Romans 9:15–16 ESV).

That concept is off-putting to some. It sounds to our human ears like selfishness or egotism. That's because we are judging by human standards. We fail to remember the nature of God. We fail to let go of our own human expectations.

There is no selfishness or egotism where God is concerned. There is no sin in God. This is why He is in control, not us.

Think about the situation for a moment. Jonah was a prophet. His mission was to bring the Word of God to others—to convert them. Yet it was only after the sailors were physically separated from Jonah that they were converted.

Sometimes even those who are called by God can be a hindrance to His message. There are times in our lives when the people we think are helping us grow closer to God are actually hurting us, and there are times when we might think we're helping others, but we are hindering them instead. A sovereign God can see this, even when we can't, and He will take action on it even if it means separation for a time.

God does things in His own way and in His own time. His ways and His timing are always perfect. God is perfection. God is love. God is pure good. There is no

selfishness or egotism where God is concerned. There is
no sin in God. This is why He is in control, not us.

*At first glance, the fish seemed to be a
vessel of destruction. But as most of us have
learned, our first impression is often not the
right impression.*

Paul wrote, "And we know that in all things God
works for the good of those who love him, who have
been called according to His purpose" (Romans 8:28
NIV).

God always holds the best interest of those who love
Him. He never slumbers, nor does He sleep. He never
stops working to bring about goodness and perfection.
Even when everything around us seems to be falling
apart in the storm, God is sovereignly working things out
for our good and His glory.

Time for the Fish

*Now the LORD provided a huge fish to swallow Jonah, and
Jonah was inside of the fish three days and three nights.*

— Jonah 1:17 NIV

In Hebrew, the word "provided" or "prepared" means
"assigned" or "delegated." It does not mean that God
created this fish specifically for Jonah, but rather that He

ordained the fish to swallow Jonah up at a selected time to carry out His plan.

At first glance, the fish seemed to be a vessel of destruction. After all, it was about to eat Jonah. That usually doesn't end well for the person being swallowed. But as most of us have learned, our first impression is often not the right impression. In this story, the ship, normally associated with safety and security, was actually the vessel of destruction.

The fish was not a vessel of destruction or a means for punishment. Rather, the fish was a vessel for salvation, for redemption, and for growth.

So what was the fish, then? Punishment? Well, some interpretations might lead us to believe that, but I don't think that's quite right, either. The storm was the punishment. It was a vicious, scary, gut-wrenching storm, which ultimately served to direct Jonah as to what he needed to do, but it also served as punishment.

The fish in this story was anointed by God. God put His own thoughts into the fish's mind, and the fish did not harm Jonah. In fact, it actually saved him from drowning.

Jonah survived in the fish's belly for three days. Miraculous indeed. But the miracle went deeper, because Jonah had time on his hands while he was in the fish.

He used that time to pray, to repent, and ultimately to bring himself closer to God. The fish was not a vessel of destruction or a means for punishment. Rather, the fish was a vessel for salvation, for redemption, and for growth.

We can emerge from the belly of the fish with a stronger faith, leaving behind those parts of ourselves that hinder us in our journey toward our supernatural destiny.

Was it a pleasant place to stay for three days and three nights? Probably not. We all know what fish smell like on the outside, right? Plus, Jonah didn't know how long he would be trapped inside the fish. Yes, God had appointed an end, but Jonah couldn't see it while he was inside the fish.

The same is true with us. We often find ourselves in unpleasant situations. But what we *think* is the vehicle of our destruction may be the vessel of our salvation.

We can't see the end, but God can. That's where faith and trust come in. We truly need to understand the sovereignty of our Lord and the unchanging fact that He works all things together for our good and His glory.

This way, when we are stuck within the belly of the fish with no end in sight, we can rest in the knowledge that God has it under control. We can emerge with a stronger faith, leaving behind those parts of ourselves that hinder us in our journey toward our supernatural destiny.

There are three elements regarding Jonah's great fish experience that merit some further analysis. Keep in mind, of course, that the giant fish represents the circumstances that God sends into your life to keep you from drowning and to redirect you back to your vocational call.

> *In order to use our gifts to serve God and fulfill our vocational calling effectively, we have to find the root of our disobedience and dig it out.*

Do we resent the fish? Most likely, yes. But when we recognize that its purpose is for our salvation, our perspective changes.

So how do we recognize our fish? We look for the three elements.

1. Confinement or Restriction

The Book of Jonah clearly states that he was inside the belly of a fish for three days and nights. There was nowhere to go. Jonah was stuck. Prior to that, while he had been in rebellion, he was on a fairly large ship with plenty of room.

He was on his way to a very large city where he would undoubtedly have freedom to move about as he pleased. But then he was confined to the space of a fish's stomach. Quite a drastic change! Not much room to move around. Jonah had no control at this point. He was completely dependent on God, the one who controlled the fish.

If you listen to God's voice rather than complaining, you will hear God whispering His plan to you, telling you about His divine will for your life.

In order to use our gifts to serve God and fulfill our vocational calling effectively, we have to find the root of our disobedience and dig it out. Only then will God release us from our "fish."

2. Solitude

Jonah was not only confined and restricted in the belly of the fish; he was also in there by himself. Solitude is different than loneliness. There are times when God must remove you from other people for a season and you will experience seclusion.

If you let yourself feel that aloneness in a painful way, it will overtake you. But if you change your focus and set your mind on God instead, your aloneness becomes solitude. It's a gift from God that allows you time to be still and listen to God as He speaks and reveals Himself in your life.

You can't experience that kind of fellowship if you interpret your aloneness as loneliness—you'll be too busy complaining about the pain of being alone. But if you listen to God's voice rather than complaining, you will hear God whispering His plan to you, telling you about His divine will for your life.

Sometimes we all need some solitude in order to reconnect with God. He has so much to say to us, but sometimes it is hard to hear Him over the sin of daily life.

Some people don't like to be alone. But the fact is, there are too many people in your ear, too many voices influencing your thoughts. In solitude, all you need is God and His voice. I'm not saying that being with people is a bad thing. Still, sometimes we all need some solitude in order to reconnect with God. He has so much to say to us, but sometimes it is hard to hear Him over the sin of daily life.

3. Unpleasantness

A fish may be a lovely creature on the outside, but the inside is another story. Jonah was not just riding on the outside of the fish: he was inside the belly. He was behind the stomach lining. He was in a smelly, slimy, damp place.

Most scholars believe that the miracle of Jonah and the fish is not necessarily the fish swallowing Jonah. Rather, the real miracle is that Jonah survived in the stomach for three days and three nights, because the stomach acids should have eaten him alive. So we know that the inside of a fish's belly is unpleasant to say the least.

Real ministry can be ugly work. It can be nasty and dirty.

God often uses the unattractive and the unpleasant as His instruments of deliverance. Placing you in such circumstances helps shape your call in life. Consider the irony of Jonah's situation: Jonah had refused to go to Nineveh in part because it was an unattractive place. So then where did he find himself? In the belly of a fish.

Real ministry can be ugly work. It can be nasty and dirty. For instance, the Bible tells us of a woman who had an issue of blood for over twelve years. She touched the hem of Christ's garment and was healed. But think— she had a continuous blood flow for twelve years. That is ugliness. Your vocational call is not going to be all glamour. It is not all about the spotlight. There will be times when you need to get your hands dirty.

Jonah's Response

Just as there are three elements to the great fish experience, there are three responses, which we see in the case of Jonah.

1. Jonah's Prayer

Then Jonah prayed to the LORD his God from inside the fish. He said, "I called out to the Lord, in my great trouble, and he answered me."

— Jonah 2:1–2 NLT

In the Old Testament, the word "Sheol" is another word for hell, but not the hell of punishment. Sheol is another word for the grave, or the place of the dead. Jonah likens the belly of the fish to a grave—he saw his time in the belly of the fish as being in a grave.

Your vocational call is not without expectations. In other words, you are expected to produce fruit. God did not give you a gift just for the sake of giving you a gift.

In a previous chapter, we discussed the concept that, for God to truly use you, you have to die to yourself. As Jesus himself taught us, "Most assuredly, I say to you, unless a grain of wheat falls into the ground and dies, it remains alone; but if it dies, it produces much grain" (John 12:24 NKJV).

Your vocational call is not without expectations. In other words, you are expected to produce fruit. God did not give you a gift just for the sake of giving you a gift. He expects you to use it to produce fruit for His Kingdom.

Don't think that just because there is a call on your life, you don't need deliverance. On the contrary, having a call on your life makes deliverance all the more necessary.

But in order for your gift to yield fruit and multiply, it must die. We must spend time in the grave in order to rise up and use our gifts to fulfill our vocational call.

When we speak of death here, we're not talking about the physical death of our bodies. We're talking about a radical transformation from what you are presently to what God intends you to be.

In order to reach that state, God has to put you in the ground. It's not a pleasant experience, but it is necessary in order for you to break that outer shell and be born into a life that will bear fruit for His Kingdom.

Just as with Jonah, you need deliverance for this process to occur. A seed can't plant itself, nor can it make itself break its shell without interacting with the soil. Jonah cried out to the Lord for deliverance. We are no different.

Don't think that just because there is a call on your life, you don't need deliverance. On the contrary, having a call on your life makes deliverance all the more necessary. In fact, your deliverance is the platform for your testimony. The grave from which you emerge is the birthplace of that testimony. That smelly, slimy, lonely belly of the fish is the very place where God is going to use you.

2. Jonah's Remembrance

When my soul fainted within me I remembered the LORD..."

— Jonah 2:7 KJV

In Hebrew the phrase "when my soul fainted" basically means to have your life turned upside down.

In other words, Jonah was saying that when his life got turned upside down by all of these events, he remembered the Lord. He brought God to mind in his solitude. He didn't waste time complaining. Instead, he started thinking about all God had been to him and done for him.

God had blessed Jonah in the past. Sometimes when we feel overwhelmed and depressed, it helps to remember what God has done for us.

Remembering won't stop the thing that we are going through, but it will restore joy.

3. Jonah's Thanksgiving

Those who pay regard to vain idols forsake their hope of steadfast love. But I with the voice of thanksgiving will sacrifice to you; what I have vowed I will pay. Salvation belongs to the LORD!"

— *Jonah 2:8–9 ESV*

Some of us might be waiting until we are released from the belly of our fish before we give thanksgiving and praise. However, Jonah offered thanksgiving while he was still in the fish's belly. That was the last element God needed to change Jonah's circumstances and set him free from the fish.

Every situation God puts us in, no matter how unpleasant, is an opportunity to reach the fulfillment of our vocational calling.

The last verse tells us that when Jonah offered praise and thanksgiving from inside the fish, God spoke to the fish and the fish spat Jonah out onto dry land.

No matter how out of control our circumstances seem, God is in control of them. Every situation God puts us in, no matter how unpleasant, is an opportunity to reach the fulfillment of our vocational calling.

Doesn't that deserve thanks and praise while we are in the moment? Why wait until we are out of the situation to offer thanksgiving if the situation itself is really a gift from God?

For some of us, God is just waiting for us to offer Him praise and thanksgiving while we are still locked in the belly of the fish. To praise means to declare with your voice. You can never praise God in silence. You can worship Him in silence, but you can never praise Him in silence. As Jonah began to declare to God, God responded to Jonah's declaration.

God responds when we offer praise and thanksgiving!

Chapter Six Questions

Question: What major storms have you experienced in the past? What storms are you experiencing now?

_____
_____
_____
_____
_____
_____
_____
_____
_____
_____
_____

Question: How are your prayer habits different during the great storms of life? How has prayer helped you through past or present storms?

_____
_____
_____
_____
_____
_____
_____

_____
_____
_____
_____

Question: What past blessings do you remember, or should you remember, when you are beset by the storms of life?

_____
_____
_____
_____
_____
_____
_____
_____
_____
_____

Action: Sometimes God puts storms in our lives because He wants us to recognize and acknowledge His sovereignty. He gives gifts to whomever He chooses, He reaps and sows as He pleases, He builds and destroys as He sees fit, and He blesses and curses as He wants. Even when everything around us seems to be falling apart in the storm, God is sovereignly working things out for our good and His glory. We truly need to understand the sovereignty of our Lord and the unchanging fact that He works all things together for our good and His glory. God responds when we offer praise and thanksgiving.

Chapter Six Notes

CHAPTER SEVEN

God Doesn't Give Up

"Arise, go to Nineveh, that great city, and preach to it the message that I tell you." So Jonah arose and went to Nineveh according to the word of the LORD. Now Nineveh was an exceedingly great city, a three-day journey in extent.

— Jonah 3:2–3 NKJV

Jonah had been spit up on dry land by the great big fish. God was now going to restore him—but something had to precede that restoration.

Deliverance and Restoration

Deliverance and restoration are two different things. To be delivered is to be transitioned out of something. To be restored is to be transitioned into something.

Paul emphasized this distinction when he said, "God has rescued us from the power of darkness and has brought us into the kingdom of his Son, whom he loves" (Colossians 1:13 GW).

Deliverance and restoration go hand in hand. If God transfers us out of something, then He will also transition us into something new. If I'm at work and I get a transfer out of one department, chances are I'm going to get transferred into another one. Deliverance without restoration is incomplete, but deliverance always comes first.

Some of us may be waiting for God to deliver us from our circumstances, but we have yet to demonstrate any true repentance.

Jonah first had to experience deliverance before he could be restored back to where he was before his disobedience. God provides deliverance, but He requires some sort of action from the person being delivered.

Jonah first had to make a decision before God delivered him. He had to take some positive action. As noted earlier, he responded in three ways: with prayer, with remembrance, and with thanksgiving. These actions spoke to the true repentance in Jonah's heart.

Some of us may be waiting for God to deliver us from our circumstances, but we have yet to demonstrate any true repentance. In that event, we could be waiting a long time for deliverance, which may never come. And without that deliverance, there can be no restoration to the path that leads us to the fulfillment of our vocational call.

According to verse nine, as Jonah sat in the belly of the big fish, he promised God, "I will pay what I have vowed."

When Jonah said, "I will pay what I have vowed," he was promising God that he would consecrate his life completely to Him. That is a pretty significant decision, is it not?

When you are going through a season of chastening and purging, the turning point always seems to revolve around a choice that you make while in the midst of your situation. When Jonah made the decision to pay the vow that he owed, he had reached his turning point.

If you're familiar with the story of the Prodigal Son, you can probably pinpoint his pivotal moment as well. If you recall the story, he was feeding slop to the pigs when he came to his senses and realized the mistakes he had made. Right then, he made the decision to return to his father and beg forgiveness.

That was his turning point. A decision was made that led to his deliverance and restoration. As with Jonah, he made a vow that preceded his deliverance.

More Than a Promise

The word "vow" is an interesting word in Hebrew. It literally refers to the act of consecration. It means to set apart, devote, or separate something or someone.

It's a matter of devoting ourselves fully to God—jumping in with both feet, not just dangling our toes in the water.

In Hebrew, the word "pay" means to bring it to completion. So when Jonah said, "I will pay what I have vowed," he was promising God that he would consecrate his life completely to Him. That is a pretty significant decision, is it not?

Oftentimes, the fact that we are going through difficult times is a sign that something big is about to happen in our lives. But we can't sit by and watch it happen. We have to participate actively in making it come about.

The question is not whether or not God can do it—He is more than able to do the miraculous—but rather: *Are we prepared to receive what He has for us?*

It's a matter of devoting ourselves fully to God—jumping in with both feet, not just dangling our toes in the water. God doesn't want divided priorities or half-hearted commitments. He wants complete devotion.

One of the biggest problems we face today is that we live compartmentalized lives. We want to devote some, but not all. We want to consecrate one part of our lives, but not the other. But we can't pick and choose. It's all or nothing where God is concerned. He doesn't want little bits and pieces of your life—He wants it all.

The point is, even when our situation seems dire, God is still in control; when we are ready, He will be there.

Another word for consecration is "sanctification." To sanctify means to set apart unto holiness for God. We can't do that only part of the way. We can't decide one part of our lives should be holy and another part shouldn't. God wants us to become His holy vessels. Of course, that doesn't mean we won't get dirty sometimes, but if we belong to God fully, then He can clean us fully.

Make no mistake: only God can deliver us. But we are the ones who need to make the decision first. God is the one who commanded the fish to spit Jonah out, but only after Jonah recommitted himself to God.

Keep in mind, too, that throughout this whole ordeal, the fish was always under God's watchful eye. God was the one who ordered the fish to swallow Jonah. He was the one who made sure Jonah would not be harmed while in its belly, and He was the one who told the fish when and where to let Jonah loose.

The point is, even when our situation seems dire, God is still in control; when we are ready, He will be there.

When you feel things spinning out of control, the Devil will plant lies in your head, insisting that God will not release you, no matter what you say or do. But God has His hand on your situation every step of the way, and His timing is perfect.

Restoration Takes Time

God restored Jonah in several ways. First, He asked Jonah once again to go to Nineveh. In so doing, God restored Jonah's original purpose. The emphasis, though, was not so much on the mandate this time, but on Jonah's response to it.

Sometimes our problem is that we want God to adjust His will to our standards. But that's not how it works.

After all, that was where the trouble had begun in the first place. But this time, it appears that Jonah had learned his lesson. He did not argue. He did not flee. He simply rose and went to Nineveh as the Lord directed. You see, the assignment never went away. It was still part of Jonah's vocational responsibility.

Sometimes our problem is that we want God to adjust His will to our standards. But that's not how it works. In Jonah's case, God did not change, nor did the assignment change. Jonah was the one who had to change.

God already knows what difficulties we will face in the assignments He gives to us. He knows our past, our present, and our future. Still, He is not going to change our assignment or lighten the load of our vocational responsibility just because we cry "uncle" and claim that it's too difficult to handle.

Sometimes God has to change our surroundings in order to elicit obedience. He has to put you outside your comfort zone.

Of course it's too difficult to handle! That's why you need God—that's the whole point of surrendering to Him. When you don't like the assignment that God has given you, just remember that God likes *you* and that He placed you in that assignment before He laid the foundations of the world.

Change of Scenery

After Jonah spent three days and three nights in the belly of the fish, he was spit out in a different location. When God originally told Jonah to go to Nineveh, Jonah was most likely in Israel. The second time, though, he was in a different place. Not only had Jonah's heart changed, but his physical location had, too.

The point is, sometimes God has to change our surroundings in order to elicit obedience. He has to put you outside your comfort zone. As we discussed earlier, when we are too comfortable with ourselves and our surroundings, we sometimes fall asleep. We become too set in our ways for God to work with us.

God demands radical obedience. If your surroundings are hindering you, He will remove you from them. We shouldn't be shocked when this happens. Instead, we should trust. The question is, are you ready for the radical, supernatural change that God has in store?

Just because we are comfortable doesn't mean we have God's favor, and just because we have God's favor doesn't mean we will feel comfortable.

Returning to Favor

When Jonah fled from Nineveh, he also fled from the face of God—from God's favor. If Jonah's flight from Nineveh also represented his flight from God's favor, it stands to reason that his return to Nineveh would also represent his return to God's favor.

Favor and comfort are not necessarily synonymous. It would be a mistake to think so. You see, we can be in a place of disobedience while we are in our comfort zone, and we can be in a place of favor with God while we are outside of our comfort zone.

Just because we are comfortable doesn't mean we have God's favor, and just because we have God's favor doesn't mean we will feel comfortable.

Paul recognized this fact when he said, "And lest I should be exalted above measure by the abundance of the revelations, a thorn in the flesh was given to me, a messenger of Satan to buffet me, lest I be exalted above measure. Concerning this thing I pleaded with the Lord three times that it might depart from me. And He said to me, 'My grace is sufficient for you, for My strength is made perfect in weakness.' Therefore most gladly I will rather boast in my infirmities, that the power of Christ may rest upon me" (2 Corinthians 12:7–9 NKJV).

When we face difficulties, God gives us the strength we need only when we come to that place of reliance.

The word "perfect" in Greek actually means "end" or "finish." Basically, Paul was saying that when we are weak, our strength reaches an end so that God's grace can take over and lift us up.

When we face difficulties, God gives us the strength we need only once we come to that place of reliance. Sometimes God restores you to a challenging situation to get you to a place where you are praying harder, fasting longer, and worshipping more fervently.

Requirement

Once God has begun the process of restoration, it should naturally lead to requirement. At the point when Jonah experienced full restoration back into his vocational responsibilities, he had to act upon that restoration for the glory of God. He was restored for a purpose and had to fulfill his vocational responsibilities as a prophet.

Through all of this, his vocational identity had never been in question. He retained his vocational identity as a prophet even while he was in disobedience.

When God gives us a mandate, it's not something we put on our to-do list or push to the back burner. It demands immediate action.

The requirement for any vocational call is obedience. For Jonah, this obedience carried with it a sense of urgency. There was a certain exigency to fulfilling the task that God had set before him. When Jonah received the instructions to rise up and go to Nineveh a second time, there was no hesitation. He rose up and went.

When God gives us a mandate, it's not something we put on our to-do list or push to the back burner. It demands immediate action. It can't wait. There's no time to worry about what you think or what other people think, or to allow anything else to stand in your way. A mandate takes priority over everything else.

Does that mean you won't face roadblocks and obstacles? Of course not. But when the mandate comes from God, He will intervene to overcome those obstacles and roadblocks. That is why it is so crucial to walk in His favor.

Just because we feel another group of people would benefit from the message God gave us doesn't mean God wants us to go to them.

God's Words, Not Yours

When God issues a mandate, it is usually quite specific, in that He sends you to a particular place or group of people. So, if you feel compelled to speak a word to a certain group of people, it doesn't mean you should speak that word to everyone you meet. To do so would be to usurp God's authority and direction. He has reasons for the tasks He assigns to you and the mandates He issues, and it is not our place to expand or diminish His directive at our own discretion.

In other words, just because we feel another group of people would benefit from the message God gave us doesn't mean God wants us to go to them.

This principle comes to light several times in the Bible. For instance, in Acts 16:6 we are told, "Paul and his companions traveled throughout the region of Phrygia and Galatia, having been kept by the Holy Spirit from preaching the word in the province of Asia" (NIV).

Although Paul and his companions wanted to go to the province of Asia to preach the message, the Holy Spirit forbade them to do so.

Compare that passage to 2 Corinthians, where Paul wrote, "Now when I went to Troas to preach the gospel of Christ and found that the Lord had opened a door for me..." (2 Corinthians 2:12 NIV).

In that instance, God opened the door for the gospel to be delivered to the people of Troas. The point is, when God requires you to fulfill a mandate, He will direct you where to go and where not to go.

The prophet does not make up his own message. It's God's message. The prophet is just the instrument through which the message is delivered.

We have to be open and obedient to His leading. That concept is made very clear in Jeremiah 1:9, which reads, "Then the LORD put forth His hand and touched my mouth, and the LORD said to me: 'Behold, I have put My words in your mouth'" (NKJV).

Here's the picture: God has a message; the prophet has a mouth. God places His message into the mouth of the prophet so that the prophet may impart that message into the hearts of the people. The prophet does not make up his own message. It's God's message. The prophet is just the instrument through which the message is delivered.

The message may impart wisdom or hope, give someone a vocational call, or confirm a vocational identity. These are not things that a mere human can do. They are directives that must come from God, and our job is to deliver those messages without getting in the way. That is the picture of true obedience to our vocational mandates.

Aside from the "where" and the "who," we have to be aware of the "how."

You might be familiar with story of Ezekiel in the valley of the dry bones. Ezekiel walked among the bones, and God said, "Prophesy to the bones. Speak to the bones and the bones will live."

As Ezekiel began to prophesy, the winds came and the bones came together and turned to living flesh (Ezekiel 37:1–9). Could a man do something like this? Of course not! The prophecy came from Ezekiel's mouth, but it was God who brought the bones to life.

Ezekiel was just the instrument through which God worked. Yet it couldn't have happened if Ezekiel was not obedient and God's favor was not upon him.

Carrying Out Our Call

Another aspect of obedience to the requirements of our call is to be conscious of *how* we carry it out. So aside from the "where" and the "who," we have to be aware of the "how."

The second time Jonah received his mandate, he arose and went to Nineveh as directed. Jonah 3:3–4 says, "Nineveh was an exceedingly great city, three days' journey in breadth. Jonah began to go into the city, going a day's journey. And he called out, 'Yet forty days, and Nineveh shall be overthrown!'" (ESV).

> *Discernment comes with spiritual maturity, and spiritual maturity comes when we surrender unconditionally to God.*

This passage tells us that Nineveh was so large that it would take Jonah three days on foot to walk from one end to the other, preaching God's message. However, we are told that he entered the city, walked for about a day, and then began proclaiming the message.

There is a lesson here for those in ministry. Jonah didn't just barge into the city and start screaming his message at people. Instead, he immersed himself in the city first (i.e., he got to know the people and the culture a little). Then he preached.

Had Jonah rushed into Nineveh and started spouting his heavy message to the first person he met, he might not have gotten the response God intended.

Sometimes in our exuberance to fulfill our vocational responsibilities, we forget to yield to God's timing and methods. We rush the situation, perhaps causing the very people we are meant to reach to turn away instead.

We might have the "where" and the "who" right, but we drop the ball on the "how." We cannot allow our own anxiousness or enthusiasm to blind us to God's direction. We have to exercise discernment as to how God wants us to carry out our task.

Discernment comes with spiritual maturity, and spiritual maturity comes when we surrender unconditionally to God. In Jonah, we see that the people responded in a positive way to Jonah's message. Jonah 3:5 recounts, "And the people of Nineveh believed God. They called for a fast and put on sackcloth, from the greatest of them to the least of them" (ESV).

Had Jonah rushed into Nineveh and started spouting his heavy message to the first person he met, he might not have gotten the response God intended. In fact, the people might've kicked him out of the city before he had walked a block.

As it was, he exercised discernment and was obedient to God not only in his destination but also in the manner in which he delivered God's message to the people.

Chapter Seven Questions

Question: In what ways have you acted disobediently toward God and then repented? What brought you to genuine repentance? In which matters or areas do you still need to repent for deliverance?

_____

_____

_____

_____

_____

_____

_____

_____

_____

_____

_____

Question: When has God changed your surroundings or circumstances to elicit your obedience? How did you seek to avoid this change? How has God's plan for you in this regard worked out so far?

_____

_____

_____

_____
_____
_____
_____
_____
_____
_____
_____

Question: When has your enthusiasm for God's Word or for your vocational calling and identity ever interfered with reaching people for Him? How? How could you have shown more discernment?

_____
_____
_____
_____
_____
_____
_____
_____
_____

Action: Some of us may be waiting for God to deliver us from our circumstances, but we have yet to demonstrate any true repentance. However, God has His hand on our situation every step of the way, and His timing is perfect. Yet He is not going to change our assignment or lighten the load of our vocational responsibility just because we cry "uncle" and claim that it's too difficult to handle.

Sometimes God has to change our surroundings in order to elicit obedience.

When we face difficulties, God gives us the strength we need only once we come to that place of reliance. There's no time to worry about what we think or what other people think, or to allow anything else to stand in our way. The prophet is just the instrument through which the message is delivered.

Furthermore, in some cases we may have the "where" and the "who" right, but we drop the ball on the "how." We cannot allow our own anxiousness or enthusiasm to blind us to God's direction. We have to exercise discernment as to how God wants us to carry out our task.

Chapter Seven Notes

CHAPTER EIGHT

Bearing Fruit

For as the rain and the snow come down from heaven and do not return there but water the earth, making it bring forth and sprout, giving seed to the sower and bread to the eater, so shall my word be that goes out from my mouth; it shall not return to me empty, but it shall accomplish that which I purpose, and shall succeed in the thing for which I sent it.

— Isaiah 55:10–11 ESV

God expects His Word to yield an abundance of good. God anoints us as farmers—our vocational *calling*—and tells us what kind of seeds we will plant—our vocational *identity*. Then He gives us instructions on where and how to plant the seeds—our vocational *responsibility*. If we neglect our duties, the seeds will not produce fruit.

The Power of God's Word

When Jonah told the people that Nineveh would be destroyed in forty days, he received a radical reaction.

All of the people, from the greatest to the smallest, repented.

Do you think Jonah would have gotten that kind of extreme reaction if the words he had spoken were his own? Doubtful. God's Word is powerful. It is designed to challenge those who receive it on the deepest level.

The power of God's Word lies in the fact that it will meet you where you are and confront you in a way that cannot be ignored.

This is how God intervenes in our lives and causes us to question the status quo. Throughout Scripture, we see God intervening in the lives of His people with signs and miracles. But more than that, we see Him intervening through His Word spoken by His prophets and messengers.

The power of God's Word lies in the fact that it will meet you where you are and confront you in a way that cannot be ignored. When God's Word confronts us, it doesn't necessarily feel good. But, as we found earlier, pain is often necessary for growth.

When we go to the doctor, we expect to receive honest answers. If there's something wrong with us, we want to know—no matter how much it might hurt.

Whether we have a broken toe, diabetes, or cancer, we want to know. It's interesting that when it comes to our physical health, we expect (even appreciate) blunt honesty, but when it comes to our spiritual health, we resent it. How can we expect to deal with a spiritual ailment unless God tells us how to fix it?

The Word of God is also designed to encourage. But even within the encouragement, there is always an implied challenge.

> *Giving praise even in the midst of the storm is obedience to God. It acknowledges that even in the worst of circumstances, God is in control of your life and you are willing to trust Him.*

Take the Psalms, for instance. While they are songs of praise, most of them were written from a place of difficulty. David wrote a number of them while he was experiencing trouble and heartache. So, aside from their uplifting messages, the Psalms also remind us that we need to worship God even in the midst of our storms.

The "Yet" Praise

Have you ever had to give God a "yet" praise? That's what I call the praises we give Him in difficult circumstances. For example, "My spouse is being unreasonable—yet I will praise God." Or, "I just lost my job—yet I will praise God."

The examples are endless, but the point is, there is no situation so dire that you can't offer a "yet" praise to

God. Now, this outlook on life is incredibly challenging. But giving praise even in the midst of the storm is obedience to God. It acknowledges that even in the worst of circumstances, God is in control of your life and you are willing to trust Him.

Jonah's simple yet powerful message conveyed that God had taken notice of their actions and He was not happy. And the people of Nineveh responded immediately.

In the Old Testament, the number forty was symbolic of a purging and a cleansing. In all likelihood, the people of Nineveh knew the significance of Jonah's proclamation right away.

Also, it's worth noting that Jonah didn't have to tell them why God was going to destroy the city in forty days. They knew they were sinning against God.

In fact, he didn't even need to tell them what to do to avert such a disaster. Jonah's simple yet powerful message conveyed that God had taken notice of their actions and He was not happy. And the people of Nineveh responded immediately.

Jonah 3:5–8 says, "Then the people of Nineveh believed in God; and they called a fast and put on sackcloth from the greatest to the least of them. When the word reached the king of Nineveh, he arose from his throne, laid aside his robe from him, covered himself with sackcloth and sat on the ashes. He issued a proclamation and it said, 'In Nineveh by the decree of the king and his nobles: Do not let man, beast, herd, or flock taste a thing. Do not let them eat or drink water. But both man and beast must be covered with sackcloth; and let men call on God earnestly that each may turn from his wicked way and from the violence which is in his hands'" (NASB).

People tend to see shame and humiliation as a bad thing. But when shame is a result of sin, it can move us to a place of true humility and real repentance, restoring favor with God.

The people of Nineveh believed God's message. The king of Nineveh stepped away from his throne, which was a symbol of relinquishing authority to God. He commanded his people to deny food and water and to put on sackcloth, which was reserved for mourning. Their self-denial served as evidence of the repentance they were experiencing inwardly. It was in their discomfort that they found favor with God.

God's Word doesn't have to be complicated to inspire repentance. However, outward actions (fasting and wearing sackcloth) should reflect inward change (genuine repentance).

Humble Pie

Andrew Murray, a well-respected missionary and author, once wrote, "The only path to humility is humiliation." Even Jesus humbled himself by dying the most humiliating death known to mankind. People tend to see shame and humiliation as a bad thing. But when shame is a result of sin, it can move us to a place of true humility and real repentance, restoring favor with God.

The character of our God is one of mercy, justice, and grace. He was true to His character when He exercised mercy as the people of Nineveh showed true repentance.

The Word of God had the power to move the Ninevites into a position of repentance, where they could then receive God's undeserved mercy. Jonah 3:10 says, "When God saw what they did, how they turned from their evil way, God relented of the disaster that he had said he would do to them, and he did not do it" (ESV).

In summary, Jonah presented the Word of God to the Ninevites. His message exposed their sin and brought them shame and humiliation. They immediately responded in humility and repentance. And because of their true repentance, God lavished mercy upon them.

Some scholars argue that this scripture is inconsistent because it indicates that God, who is immutable, actually changed His mind with regard to the destruction of

Nineveh. More accurately, though, it was not God who changed His mind, but the people who changed their minds and their actions.

The character of our God is one of mercy, justice, and grace. He was true to His character when He exercised mercy as the people of Nineveh showed true repentance.

Had the Ninevites continued on their course, unfazed by God's Word, the outcome would have been very different. No mercy would have been merited; He would have exercised justice instead.

God did not change. The people did.

Chapter Eight Questions

Question: How have you experienced the intervention of God's Word in your life? Was it painful? Did you find yourself humbled—even humiliated?

_____

_____

_____

_____

_____

_____

_____

_____

_____

_____

Question: How have you witnessed the intervention of God's Word in others' lives as a result of you living out your vocational responsibilities? Did it seem painful for those God reached through you?

_____

_____

_____

_____

_____

_____

_____

_____

_____

_____

_____

Question: What praises could you offer God during the storms you are experiencing in your life right now?

_____

_____

_____

_____

_____

_____

_____

_____

_____

_____

Action: God anoints us as farmers—our vocational *calling*—and tells us what kind of seeds we will plant—our vocational *identity*. Then He gives us instructions on where and how to plant the seeds—our vocational *responsibility*. If we neglect our duties, the seeds will not produce fruit.

The Word of God had the power to move people into a position of repentance, where they can then receive God's undeserved mercy. His message doesn't have to be complicated to inspire repentance. However, when

God's Word confronts us, it doesn't necessarily feel good. Pain is often necessary for growth.

Giving praise even in the midst of the storm is obedience to God. It acknowledges that even in the worst of circumstances, God is in control of your life and you are willing to trust Him.

Chapter Eight Notes

_____

_____

_____

_____

_____

_____

_____

_____

_____

_____

_____

_____

_____

_____

_____

_____

_____

_____

_____

_____

_____

_____

_____

_____

CHAPTER NINE

Our Real Motivations

But it displeased Jonah exceedingly, and he was angry. And He prayed to the LORD and said, "O LORD, is not this what I said when I was yet in my country? That is why I made haste to flee to Tarshish; for I knew that you are a gracious God and merciful, slow to anger and abounding in steadfast love, and relenting from disaster. Therefore now, O LORD, please take my life from me, for it is better for me to die than to live." And the LORD said, "Do you do well to be angry?"

— Jonah 4:1–4 ESV

For all intents and purposes, the task Jonah performed was a success. He declared God's Word to the Ninevites, and they repented. But then the story takes a strange twist. Jonah, who should have been happy over the success of his ministry, was angry because God had forgiven the people of Nineveh. So angry, in fact, that he wanted God to take his life.

The story tells us that Jonah was "exceedingly displeased." In Hebrew, the literal translation is "totally disgusted." Why would that be?

Keeping It Real

To help us understand Jonah's rather strange reaction, let's look at 1 Peter 4:7–11, which states, "The end of all things is at hand; therefore be self-controlled and sober-minded for the sake of your prayers. Above all, keep loving one another earnestly, since love covers a multitude of sins. Show hospitality to one another without grumbling. As each has received a gift, use it to serve one another, as good stewards of God's varied grace: whoever speaks, as one who speaks oracles of God; whoever serves, as one who serves by the strength that God supplies—in order that in everything God may be glorified through Jesus Christ. To him belong glory and dominion forever and ever. Amen" (ESV).

If we are not serious about our mandate—if we're not serious about our call and if we're not serious about what we're supposed to be doing in life—then we might actually be a hindrance to others who are serious.

In this passage, Peter was talking about those who have a vocational calling. He started the passage by telling us that time is short, so there's none to waste on pettiness or backbiting. He was instructing us to be serious about our life and about our ministry—to use our gifts wisely, without complaining, in service to others.

If we are not serious about our mandate—if we're not serious about our call and if we're not serious about what we're supposed to be doing in life—then we might actually be a hindrance to others who are serious.

God gives us the seeds, and the seeds are our gift to be planted in the soil to produce fruit. But He also gives us the hoe and the rake and the watering can—the tools we need to plant the seeds and allow them to grow and bear fruit.

We've all heard the adage that if we're not part of the solution, then we're part of the problem. That holds very true when it comes to following our vocational call. Earlier we mentioned the sense of urgency that accompanies a mandate from God. We should all start feeling that sense of urgency in our callings.

And no calling can be accomplished effectively without three factors: self-control (watchfulness over our actions), sober-mindedness (taking things seriously), and prayer (our connection to God).

When we are saved, we each receive a gift from the Spirit. However, our gifts are not for ourselves, but for others. Peter told us that we need to use them wisely in the fulfillment of our vocational call.

As mentioned earlier, God gives us our gifts to use in His service, but He also gives us the tools to make those gifts fruitful. To elaborate on the analogy made earlier, God gives us the seeds, and the seeds are our gift to be planted in the soil to produce fruit. But He also gives us the hoe and the rake and the watering can—the tools we need to plant the seeds and allow them to grow and bear fruit.

Jonah did not exercise self-control. He got caught up in his own pettiness and his own jealousy.

Unless we use our gifts wisely and prayerfully, we may not have access to the tools we need to complete our tasks.

Keep the Goal in Mind

Jonah's ministry yielded good fruit, but at the end of the day, it was flawed. Why? Because Jonah did not stay watchful against his own actions. He was flawed, just like the rest of us.

It goes back to what Peter was saying. Jonah did not exercise self-control. He got caught up in his own pettiness and his own jealousy. He complained and grumbled, still floundering in his own expectations as to how things should have gone. He focused on his own desires instead of God's.

Ministry itself should never take precedence over the people to whom we are ministering. When ministry becomes a goal in and of itself, it results in an unhealthy situation. The goal of ministry should be to produce fruit for God's Kingdom.

Unless we keep that goal in mind, problems seep in. That's what happened to Jonah. Instead of rejoicing in God's mercy to Nineveh, he got caught up in his own petty jealousies.

In a foxhole, soldiers are not thinking about themselves: They are thinking about protecting the unit as a whole.

God did not send Jonah to Nineveh for the sheer purposes of delivering a message. Rather, He sent him to deliver a people. At times, we tend to put process over people, but that's not how God operates. Process drives ministries to serve people, but God's primary focus is the people, not the process.

Further, ministry cannot be done in isolation. Not only is it about people, but people also carry it out. A seed grows into a plant, which produces fruit, which in turn produces more seeds. It's not an isolated process. Ministry needs people in order to function and grow. It cannot be done in seclusion.

In a way, we need to adopt a military mindset. In a foxhole, soldiers are not thinking about themselves: They are thinking about protecting the unit as a whole. They may not know or like the other people in the foxhole, but they protect one another.

Hidden Motives

As the story of Jonah comes to a close, we learn the real reason he didn't obey the Lord and go to Nineveh the first time. Jonah 4:2 says, "Ah, LORD, was not this what I said when I was still in my country? Therefore I fled previously to Tarshish; for I know that You are a gracious and merciful God, slow to anger and abundant in lovingkindness, One who relents from doing harm" (NKJV).

We must stay constantly vigilant and self-controlled. We must continually check and double-check our motives in our ministry.

Originally, we may have thought Jonah fled to Tarshish because he was afraid to go to Nineveh, or perhaps worried that his ministry wouldn't be successful there. But it turns out that he didn't think the people in Nineveh deserved God's mercy and forgiveness.

He was also very jealous. Up until that point, God only chose the Israelites; thus, they were the primary benefactors of His loving-kindness. Perhaps he wanted to keep it that way. Perhaps he didn't want others, especially the Ninevites, to undermine the status of the Israelites or take advantage of God's great mercy and grace.

How does this relate to us in the pursuit of our vocational call? As Peter said, it means that we must stay constantly vigilant and self-controlled. We must continually check and double-check our motives in our ministry.

Are we doing things out of jealousy? Self-righteousness? Conceit? Self-importance? Unless we stay constantly watchful regarding the focus of our ministry, we run the risk of falling into the same trap that Jonah did.

No matter what vocational calling God has assigned to us, there is one common denominator: We must use our gifts to serve God and others.

Chapter Nine Questions

Question: What are your goals and motivations in your calling? What fruit are you producing for God's Kingdom? How well is your fruit for the Kingdom aligned with your goals?

_____

_____

_____

_____

_____

_____

_____

_____

_____

_____

_____

Question: What tools has God given you to live out your vocational responsibilities, and how do you use them? What people has God put in your life to help you produce fruit for His Kingdom?

_____

_____

_____

_____

_____

_____

_____

_____

_____

_____

_____

Question: How is your pursuit of your calling focused on other people, rather than on yourself or on other objectives? Are there any ways in which you are not focused on reaching people for God?

_____

_____

_____

_____

_____

_____

_____

_____

_____

Action: The goal of ministry should be to produce fruit for God's Kingdom. If we are not serious about our mandate—if we're not serious about our call and if we're not serious about what we're supposed to be doing in life—then we might actually be a hindrance to others who are serious. And unless we use our gifts wisely and prayerfully, we may not have access to the tools we need to complete our tasks.

Ministry cannot be done in isolation. Not only is it about people, but people also carried it out. Unless we stay constantly watchful regarding the focus of our ministry, we run the risk of falling into the same traps of pettiness and jealousy as Jonah did.

Chapter Nine Notes

_____

_____

_____

_____

_____

_____

_____

_____

_____

_____

_____

_____

_____

_____

_____

_____

_____

_____

_____

_____

_____

_____

_____

_____

_____

CHAPTER TEN

God's Will > Our Plan

Jonah went out of the city and sat to the east of the city and made a booth for himself there. He sat under it in the shade, till he should see what would become of the city. Now the LORD God appointed a plant and made it come up over Jonah, that it might be a shade over his head, to save him from his discomfort. So Jonah was exceedingly glad because of the plant. But when dawn came up the next day, God appointed a worm that attacked the plant, so that it withered. When the sun rose, God appointed a scorching east wind, and the sun beat down on the head of Jonah so that he was faint. And he asked that he might die and said, "It is better for me to die than to live." But God said to Jonah, "Do you do well to be angry for the plant?" And he said, "Yes, I do well to be angry, angry enough to die." And the LORD said, "You pity the plant, for which you did not labor, nor did you make it grow, which came into being in a night and perished in a night. And should not I pity Nineveh, that great city, in which there are more than 120,000 persons who do not know their right hand from their left, and also much cattle?"

— Jonah 4:5–11 ESV

Jonah's main problem, and the problem so many of us face in ministry, was misplaced expectations. As we've said before, God cannot be controlled or manipulated. He does as He pleases.

Because of that, His actions oftentimes don't mesh with our expectations. Yet we so often forget that the true pursuit of our vocational calling requires the abandonment of our expectations.

We can't understand everything that God does, nor can we discern His reasons. That's why He wants us to rest our minds and trust in His character.

Complete submission to God's will involves letting go of our self-centered motives and expectations and, instead, relinquishing them to God. When we fail to do that, we set ourselves up for disappointment. Left unchecked, that disappointment can lead to despair, which paralyzes us in the pursuit of our ministry.

Our human nature is prone to judgment. Yet, like Jonah, even though we cannot see what God sees in other people, we are called to minister to them.

We can't understand everything that God does, nor can we discern His reasons. That's why He wants us to rest our minds and trust in His character. Many times, though, our human nature gets in the way and we start to second-guess His ways.

We think, "Why should I minister to those people? They don't care about God." Or, "Do I really have to visit murderers and thieves in prison? They are such awful people." Or, "Why should I let those people into the food pantry? They have jobs and can buy their own food."

Since we are sinners, thoughts like these are bound to run through our minds. But God doesn't give up on us, just as He didn't give up on Jonah.

Many times when we experience anger, we are really angry with ourselves.

After Jonah finished with his vocational responsibilities, he became angry. He cried out, "'Therefore now, O LORD, please take my life from me, for it is better for me to die than to live.' And the LORD said, 'Do you do well to be angry?'" (Jonah 4:3–4 ESV)

Now, there's nothing wrong with anger in certain circumstances, but in this case, Jonah's anger was misplaced. In fact, he probably didn't even know the full reason as to why he was angry. Was he angry with the Ninevites for turning from their sinful ways? Was he angry with God for His merciful nature? Or perhaps he was angry with himself for yielding to his own selfish expectations.

Many times when we experience anger, we are really angry with ourselves. Ministry can be unpredictable to say the least, and many times things don't go as we planned or expected. That makes us mad. Yet, rather than admit to the real cause of our anger, we project it onto God, the church, and our ministry. Unfortunately, that only makes matters worse, because we can't really justify our anger, so we just sink deeper into a funk.

This happened to Jonah. Not only did he get depressed and give up, but he also disengaged himself from the people to whom he was called to minister. He built himself a shelter and sat outside of the city perimeter.

Jonah had no trouble accepting God's mercy and grace when He was pouring it out on him. But he did, however, have a problem when it was being poured out onto those he didn't like.

It may seem like a silly thing to have done, but anger makes us do silly things, doesn't it? Also, keep in mind that Jonah was probably still hoping that his little temper tantrum might cause God to reconsider destroying the city.

He was sitting close enough to the city to see what happened, but far enough away so that he wouldn't suffer the fallout should God decide to destroy Nineveh after all.

Your Standards Matter

Jonah also had inconsistent standards. After God challenged Jonah about his anger, He provided for him a plant that gave him shade from the hot sun.

God created the plant out of nothing to protect Jonah—not because of anything Jonah did, but out of His own mercy and grace. Jonah was very glad about this. Once again, God had delivered him. He had delivered him from a storm, from the raging sea, and from the belly of a fish, and now He delivered him from the scorching sun.

We may be doing all the right things on the surface, but it is only a matter of time before the foundation collapses and the sin underneath is exposed.

Jonah had no trouble accepting God's mercy and grace when He was pouring it out on him. But he did, however, have a problem when it was being poured out onto those he didn't like. Jonah wanted to pick and choose those to whom God offered His deliverance.

This is a clear example of double standards in ministry. If we begin to pick and choose who should receive the benefits of our calling, then we destroy the purpose God intended. It is not for us to determine who should receive the benefit of our spiritual gifts.

We may be doing all the right things on the surface, but it is only a matter of time before the foundation collapses and the sin underneath is exposed. Jonah had already done exactly what God had wanted him to do, but his heart was angry and bitter, reverting him back into a state of disobedience.

Remember the Plant

Consider the plant that God provided for Jonah. Jonah had made a shelter for himself, but for some reason, the shelter was incomplete and Jonah's head was exposed to the glaring sun.

What are you waiting on God to do? And how long have you been waiting? Could it be that He is waiting on you?

God created a plant out of nothing in a desert place where plants don't usually grow. He provided it in a blink. It didn't grow over time like a normal plant, but was immediately there and large enough to provide shade.

He did this even though Jonah had a sinful heart. He protected Jonah, not abandoning him as He could have. Keep in mind that Jonah had taken some action first in building the shelter, but he couldn't quite finish it to the point where it would protect him completely. God filled in where Jonah was lacking.

In our lives, even when a situation we face seems hopeless, we need to remember the plant. God created it out of nothing. He created a solution to a problem when there was none in sight. He had complete control of the situation. He protected Jonah when Jonah was unable to help himself, even though Jonah was in a state of disobedience. He will do the same for you, but it may require some action on your part.

What are you waiting on God to do? And how long have you been waiting? Could it be that He is waiting on you? Perhaps He is just waiting for you to make a move, to make a start, and He will fill in where you are unable. The keys are faith and trust.

Was God playing games with Jonah? Never! But we can be sure that He was teaching him some valuable lessons.

Keep Your Priorities Straight

We've already seen how Jonah struggled with some pretty significant character flaws. In these last verses of the story, we see God revealing even more about Jonah in regard to his vocational calling.

Understandably, Jonah was glad when the plant appeared and shaded his head. He was also understandably upset when the plant died, taking away the shade he was enjoying.

Was God playing games with Jonah? Never! But we can be sure that He was teaching him some valuable lessons. It's evident that Jonah was concerned about all of the wrong things. The only time we see Jonah get happy about something is when the plant appears to shade his head. He didn't seem glad at all that an entire city of men, women, children and cattle had just been spared from destruction. Quite the opposite—he was angry.

It's hard to believe, but Jonah actually had pity for the plant, which he did not create—yet he *did not* have pity for the people for whom he labored in his ministry.

Do we spend our time worrying about the temporary—that which will come and go in a blink—or do we spend our time concerned with things of a more substantial nature—things that really matter?

Perhaps part of his emotional attachment to the plant was because it was providing him with the benefit of shade. Still, we might think he'd have more of an emotional reaction to the proposed death of thousands of people than to the demise of a plant!

Before we judge Jonah too harshly, though, aren't we like that sometimes? Take money, for example. On those rare occasions when we have cash in our pockets, how anxious are we to part with it?

We are generally very reluctant to hand over our hard-earned cash. Yet there are people all around the world who need food, shelter, clothes, medicine, education, and so on. Still, we tend to keep our money in our pockets. Do we care more about inanimate objects than about people?

What Are You Worried About?

One of the biggest marks of spiritual maturity is where you choose to expend your energy. Do we spend our time worrying about the temporary—that which will come and go in a blink—or do we spend our time concerned with things of a more substantial nature—things that really matter? Jesus teaches us the difference.

We get so focused on the storms in our lives—the events that come and go—that we lose sight of the miraculous, the eternal, and the real purpose for our being.

In Matthew 8:24, He was with His disciples in a boat when an unexpected storm came up. The disciples were worried, but Jesus was asleep in the bow. Why? Didn't He care about the well-being of His disciples?

Jesus was mature enough to realize that the storm was a temporary thing, and thus was nothing to get emotionally distraught about.

Compare this to Mark 6:30, which tells the story of how Jesus fed the multitude with a few loaves and fish. Jesus expressed concern this time—for the people.

He performed one of His best-known miracles so that the people would be fed. Then, right after that story in Mark 6:45, a new narrative begins.

After Jesus fed the multitudes, some disciples got caught in a storm again. They saw Jesus walking on the water toward them, but even so, they were frightened. They had forgotten all about the miracle of the loaves and fish. They had not learned their lesson. Once again, they were worried about the fleeting storm, failing to focus on the miraculous act that Jesus had just performed.

Without compassion, we can easily fall into the trap of apathy.

We fall into the same trap many times ourselves. We get so focused on the storms in our lives—the events that come and go—that we lose sight of the miraculous, the eternal, and the real purpose for our being.

In the case of Jonah, he was clearly focused on the temporal, not the eternal. As a result, he lacked compassion for the people of Nineveh.

Compassion is a vital component to an effective ministry, and we all must have it.

I Feel for You

Some people are very gifted in ministry, but they lack compassion. They are very clinical in their approach to ministry. While they are able to fulfill their vocational responsibilities, they lack heart.

To reach our potential fully, however, we must have compassion for others. Compassion is different than pity. You can have pity on someone from an emotional distance. Compassion indicates more of a connection.

In fact, the word "compassion" essentially means "to cover someone in their weakness." God saw Nineveh's repentance and had compassion on them by covering them.

How do we speak deliverance to people whose worldview is so jaded that it has become part of their psyche? How do we cover those people?

Without compassion, we can easily fall into the trap of apathy. Jonah was apathetic to the plight of the Ninevites because he lacked compassion and empathy for them. No ministry can endure if it isn't rooted in compassion for others.

As 1 Peter 3:8 says, "Finally, all of you should be of one mind. Sympathize with each other. Love each other as brothers and sisters. Be tenderhearted, and keep a humble attitude" (NLT).

God told Jonah that his ministry must have compassion. He indicated that the people of Nineveh didn't know their left hand from their right hand, meaning they didn't know right from wrong. Perhaps that is the very reason Jonah disliked them.

What about us? How do we speak deliverance to people whose worldview is so jaded that it has become part of their psyche? How do we cover those people?

With compassion.

Chapter Ten Questions

Question: How are your standards for yourself and others the same? How are they different? How can you bring your expectations for yourself and those for others in line?

_____
_____
_____
_____
_____
_____
_____
_____
_____
_____

Question: Where do you expend your energy? What do you spend time thinking or worrying about?

_____
_____
_____
_____
_____

————————————————
————————————————
————————————————
————————————————
————————————————
————————————————

Question: In what ways do you show compassion for others? How could you show greater compassion, and to whom?

————————————————
————————————————
————————————————
————————————————
————————————————
————————————————
————————————————
————————————————
————————————————
————————————————

Action: Complete submission to God's will involves letting go of our self-centered motives and expectations and instead relinquishing them to God. When we fail to do that, we set ourselves up for disappointment. We may be doing all the right things on the surface, but it is only a matter of time before the foundation collapses and the sin underneath is exposed.

We become so focused on the storms in our lives—the events that come and go—that we lose sight of the miraculous, the eternal, and the real purpose for our being. Perhaps God is just waiting for us to make a move, to make a start, and He will fill in where we are unable. To reach our potential fully, however, we must have compassion for others.

Chapter Ten Notes

CONCLUSION

Pursuing Our Call

Our God is a God of compassion, and if we are not displaying that compassion to the world, then we are not true ambassadors of Christ.

There will be pain, but God's love for you knows no bounds. He has a miraculous life planned out for you.

Jonah missed the point. He was angry about the wrong things. In Chapter Four, God is trying to instruct Jonah. The plant, the worm, the east wind—they were all designed by God as teaching tools. God needed to expose some things in Jonah in order to bring him more in line with the character of God.

There are situations and circumstances in our lives that God will use as teaching tools for us. I have come to fully believe that tumultuous situations are really God's training ground for how to walk in His anointing.

He may provide conditions that challenge us, as He did with the plant and the worm, or He may use a situation you've already gotten yourself into, like when Jonah was on the boat to Tarshish.

By giving your life to a sovereign God, you lose nothing and gain everything.

These situations may seem harsh, but they are opportunities for growth. There will be pain, but God's love for you knows no bounds. He has a miraculous life planned out for you. He has anointed you with a vocational identity and has given you vocational responsibilities that will result in the supernatural.

By giving your life to a sovereign God, you lose nothing and gain everything.

You are on the edge of a revolution—a paradigm shift of epic proportions.

God will never stop pursuing you. He wants you to have real joy and fulfillment in your life.

So, turn to Him right now and open your heart to His divine calling for you.

His will is so much greater than your plan.

Acknowledgements

I am eternally grateful for all of those whom God has sovereignly placed in my life, who were instrumental in the formation of my vocational call and identity.

I am grateful for my mother, Janice Moore, who, as a single mother, raised me and gave me every opportunity to grow and expand as a person.

I acknowledge my "spiritual mother," Dr. Lydia Jackson Waters. She gave me a love for worship, was the first to recognize the vocational call in my life, and opened doors for me to begin operating in that call.

I praise God for brother Ronald Lowe, the Sunday school teacher who shared the gospel with me and led me to the Lord at the age of nine.

I have been blessed to walk with some amazing men who serve as both friends and accountability brothers:

To Bishop Sheriden McDaniel, Elder Marc Little, Pastor Garth Gilliam, and Pastor Royce Porter—thank you for the years of friendship and time invested in me as a person. I am especially grateful for Pastor De'Andre Salter, who is my prayer partner; and Pastor Bryan Loritts, that friend who "sticketh closer than a brother" and has helped me navigate through the murky parts of life and wrestled with me on the deep things of Scripture. My iron has been sharpened by you both.

I am grateful for the counsel and leadership insight of Dr. Larry Titus.   His ability to speak words of encouragement into me cannot be quantified with mere words.

I must thank Praise Tabernacle Bible Church, which was the creative crucible for this work. I could not have asked to shepherd a better congregation. You created a safe environment for me to work out the proverbial kinks in my vocational call.

To the elders, both past and present, who have walked with me and given me counsel, I am grateful.

For my father-in-law, Bishop Kenneth C. Ulmer, who is both my spiritual father and pastoral covering, I am also thankful. He became a father to the fatherless for me, and he has inspired me and enlarged my vision of the Kingdom. I thank him for having the vision to plant the ministry that gave birth to this work. I am grateful to him for leading me into spiritual manhood.

Lastly, to my wife, Keniya Carmel Ulmer-Moore, who has walked by my side for sixteen years, I offer my deep appreciation. God loved me enough to place her in my life as a sign of His grace toward me. If grace is God giving us what we do not deserve, then Keniya is the manifestation of that grace. She is my life's partner, and for that I praise God!

Notes

1. Thomas Paine. *The Age of Reason*, 1807.
2. Russell Kirk. "The Moral Imagination." *Literature and Belief* (vol. 1), 1981, 37–49.

About the Author

Educated at Talbot School of Theology, Jody D. Moore currently serves as the Senior Pastor-Teacher at Praise Tabernacle Bible Church in the City of Chino, California. He has held executive leadership roles both in ministry and in several Fortune 500 companies. He specializes in leadership development and organizational assessment. He has served on the boards of several non-profits. Pastor Jody resides in Southern California with his wife and three daughters.

About SermonToBook.Com

SermonToBook.com began with a simple belief: that sermons should be touching lives, *not* collecting dust. That's why we turn sermons into high-quality books that are accessible to people all over the globe.

Turning your sermon series into a book exposes more people to God's Word, better equips you for counseling, accelerates future sermon prep, adds credibility to your ministry, and even helps make ends meet during tight times.

John 21:25 tells us that the world itself couldn't contain the books that would be written about the work of Jesus Christ. Our mission is to try anyway. Because, in Heaven, there will no longer be a need for sermons or books. Our time is now.

If God so leads you, we'd love to work with you on your sermon or sermon series.

Visit www.sermontobook.com to learn more.

Encourage the Author by Reviewing This Book

If you've found this book helpful or challenging, the author would love your honest feedback. Please consider stopping by Amazon.com and writing a review.

To submit a review, simply go to *God's Will > Your Plan*'s Amazon.com page, click "Write a customer review" in the Customer Reviews section, and click to submit.

Made in United States
Orlando, FL
26 November 2021

10759489R00104